CAROLE MAYHALL

HELP LORD

MY WHOLE LIFE HURTS

NAVPRESS

A MINISTRY OF THE NAVIGATORS
P.O. BOX 6000, COLORADO SPRINGS, COLORADO 80934

The Navigators is an international Christian organization. Jesus Christ gave His followers the Great Commission to go and make disciples (Matthew 28:19). The aim of The Navigators is to help fulfill that commission by multiplying laborers for Christ in every nation.

NavPress is the publishing ministry of The Navigators. NavPress publications are tools to help Christians grow. Although publications alone cannot make disciples or change lives, they can help believers learn biblical discipleship, and apply what they learn to their lives and ministries.

First printing, paperback edition, 1990

Scripture quotations in this publication are from the *Holy Bible: New International Version* (NIV). Copyright © 1973, 1978, 1984, International Bible Society. Used by permission of Zondervan Bible Publishers. Other versions quoted include *The Living Bible* (TLB), © 1971 by Tyndale House Publishers, Wheaton, Illinois. Used by permission; The *New American Standard Bible* (NASB), © The Lockman Foundation 1960, 1962, 1963, 1968, 1971, 1973, 1975, 1977; and the *King James Version* (KJV).

Printed in the United States of America

FOR A FREE CATALOG OF
NAVPRESS BOOKS & BIBLE STUDIES,
CALL TOLL FREE 800-366-7788 (USA)
or 1-416-499-4615 (CANADA)

CONTENTS

AUTHOR

Carole Mayhall often prays, "Lord, don't let me talk beyond my *walk*." Because of this prayer, she takes a personal, practical, and biblical approach in her writing and thinks of each of her books as being a slice of her life as she learns lessons from God.

Carole and her husband, Jack, have been with The Navigators since 1956, living in California and Illinois and for the last fifteen years in Colorado Springs.

Jack has had a variety of responsibilities over the years including seven years as the United States Director. Currently they are ministering with The Navigators in the department of Marriage and the Family and travel extensively in the United States and overseas speaking to individuals and groups concerning marriage and discipleship.

Carole is the author of several books, including *Lord of My Rocking Boat* and *Words That Hurt, Words That Heal*. She has co-authored with Jack *Marriage Takes More Than Love*, and *Opposites Attack*.

To my mother-in-law,
Ruth Mayhall,
a very courageous woman

The LORD will accomplish what
concerns me; Thy lovingkindness,
O LORD, is everlasting; do not forsake
the works of Thy hands.
                    (Psalm 138:8, NASB)

A book about God's methods of
stripping away life's supports in
order that we may learn to trust in
Him alone.

PREFACE

The narrow cobblestone streets echoed with the excited laughter of children making their way to the picturesque plaza in quaint Guanajuato, Mexico. Small, hastily erected stalls displayed hundreds of painted candies in the shapes of donkeys, skeletons, and skulls as the children, escorted by teachers and parents, carefully selected their favorite candies for this Day of the Dead Halloween holiday.

On this bright day, our granddaughter, Sunny, age five, was anything but sunny. She drooped sadly at home, her right leg encased in a plaster cast from hip to toe—the result of a fall several days before that cracked both the large and small bones of her lower leg. Sunny was not yet proficient at maneuvering with her two small crutches, and Lynn, her mother, was unable to carry her through the streets and plaza to enable her to shop with her class.

Sobbing on Lynn's shoulder over this major disappointment, Sunny looked pathetically at her mother and whimpered, "My *life* hurts more than my leg!"

Sunny's perceptive lament reflects the aching of many hearts. We take in stride the single pain of an area in our lives that begins to hurt. But when an avalanche of problems slams down the mountain to bury us, trapping us helplessly beneath, we cry plaintively, "Lord, my *life* hurts!"

Yet God controls the avalanche. It can be His way to deliberately, methodically strip away that which will hinder us from knowing Him deeply. The force of an avalanche strips away supports we've counted on, often leaving us with nothing. Nothing, that is, but God Himself.

The divine axe has fallen.

Blow by horrible blow, I watch as the support limbs of my friend's life are hacked away.

Whack! And her effervescent mother lies dying and wasted.

Whomp! And her own health deteriorates into chronic back problems and then diabetes.

Wham! And her lovely unmarried daughter gives birth to a baby to raise in her parents' home—a baby yellowed with jaundice, bruised—who almost doesn't make it through the first week.

Crash! And debts pile high from doctor and hospital bills, the plight of a mother, daughter, and grandson without insurance.

Whop! Bam! Whish! Irritations escalate, doubts rise high, things break, rest is nonexistent, and life becomes a nightmare of pain and frustration. Before my eyes I see my friend stripped to the bare bones of her trust as the divine axe falls again and again.

She's reeling from the blows. Numb and bewildered. I watch and cry.

Max Lucado has written,

> The rubber of faith meets the road of reality
> under hardship . . . the trueness of one's belief
> is revealed in pain. Genuineness and character
> are unveiled in misfortune. Faith is at its best,
> not in three-piece suits on Sunday mornings or
> at VBS on summer days, but at hospital bed-
> sides, cancer wards, and cemeteries.[1]

My friend has experienced this literally. Her faith is meeting the road to reality this very minute. The bumps and potholes jar her, the twists and turns confuse her, the seeming endlessness of the journey leaves her baffled.

God has vast, deliberate means at His disposal to fashion, mold, and conform us to the likeness of His Son. Sometimes the lessons strike like lightning, leaving us in shock and asking, "What happened?" At other times the trials ooze like mud between the cracks of life so slowly we are unaware of them, until we stop long enough amid the pressures of life to realize we are covered with slime.

To be ignorant of God's processes may be to question His love. When God strips us, we are inclined to ask, "What did I do to incur His wrath? Has He cast me aside?" Or we say, "Perhaps I've been wrong all along to trust His goodness."

I am not writing about ordinary trials, but about the multiplied pains and problems that occur simultaneously or in quick succession only a few times in most lives. Such experiences are tools in God's hands to strip away the supports of our lives—to tear them from beneath us so that we might realize our support must rest in God *alone.*

This book is an attempt to explore some of God's creative measures so that as Christians we may understand what is happening when we face "trials of many kinds" (James 1:2).

We will examine the despair, isolation, confusion, numbness, doubt, and rejection that often result from His stripping processes, along with some ideas about how to survive those times. Then we will look at His purpose for it all.

At the end of this book, I have included a section for personal Bible study: the "Personal Application and Reflection" section. These questions can be used to delve deeper into biblical principles relevant to the stripping process.

As you read each chapter of the book, please use these studies to whatever extent meets your need. You can scan the questions to stimulate thought or use them as a starting point for further research of the aspects in your unique experience.

If we are learners—disciples—and wholly at His disposal to learn the lessons of life, we will welcome His fashioning as from a friend who loves us and knows what is best for us at all times.

NOTE:
1. Max Lucado, *No Wonder They Call Him the Savior* (Portland: Multnomah, 1986), page 77.

ACKNOWLEDGMENT

So much of my husband's thinking and study has gone into this book, that it is hard for me to tell where he leaves off and I begin! In fact, his input has been so great that I wanted to list him as co-author of this book, but he objected.

To say that I couldn't have written it without him is true. But it's not enough. Jack's contribution to my life continues to be incalculable. So, even though he asked that he not be listed as an author, please know that many of the lessons shared in this book have come from God through Jack to me.

AN ALLEGORY

Everything about the small boy drooped. His hair, usually sticking out in all directions, lay limp around his pale face. Even his freckles seemed in danger of sliding off his down-turned expression. He looked as if he'd lost his best friend. And he had.

For a moment his grandmother stood silently at the back door, watching the dejected figure who sat on the top step of the porch, his chin resting on his palms. Then, brushing the back of her hand across her eyes as she went to him, she folded her large frame to sit beside him and put her arm around his slight shoulders.

"You'll miss Daddy." The words came out briskly, masking the shakiness of her voice.

Silently, he nodded, his lips trembling.

She cleared her throat and swallowed. *He's only*

nine, she thought. *He's big enough to know, but too small to comprehend.* The memory of the day before, when they stood by the casket in the cemetery, caused her to blink back tears once again.

"Want me to tell you a story?"

It had been a thing between them from the time he could speak. "Story," he'd say, his eyes wide with anticipation, and she loved to comply.

Mutely, he shrugged, glancing listlessly toward her.

She pretended not to notice his apathy and began: "Once, long ago and far away . . ." He loved her to begin this way, but today his dull eyes remained fixed on a spot of ground three feet away.

" . . . in a land called Nun, there was a prince whose father, the king, grew very ill. The prince called in every doctor in the kingdom . . ."

Johnny flicked a glance sideways, then looked back to the ground.

". . . but, though they did all they could, the king died. The prince was so sad that, at first, he couldn't do anything at all. Then he became angry at the death angel who had taken his father away. Depression followed his anger, and the prince began to wonder if he would ever be happy again.

"*Does life consist of nothing but living and working and dying?* the prince thought. *Where is meaning? Where is happiness?* the prince agonized in his thoughts.

"He called all the wise men of his kingdom together and asked them his questions, but the wise men only pulled at their beards and shook their heads. The prince continued to grow more and more depressed.

"Finally he said to his mother, 'I'm going on a

search throughout my whole kingdom to find if there is any happiness and meaning in life. If there is, I'll come back and rule the kingdom, but if there isn't, I'll never come back. For how can I lead a people if there is no hope and if life consists only of working and dying?'

"'I understand, my son,' his mother **said**. 'But before you go, let me give you a gift.' She hunted in a huge wardrobe and pulled from the farthest corner, a little box. When the prince opened the box, he found a small piece of what looked like plain glass. He raised his eyebrows in question.

"His mother smiled. 'No my son, this is no ordinary piece of glass. It is a magic glass. When you look at someone through it, you will see him in a future state. It may help you in your quest.'

"The glass seemed a rather useless object to the prince, but being a polite young man, he thanked his mother, kissed her goodbye, and started on his search."

Johnny's gaze was no longer on the ground. A glint shone deep in his eyes as he stared into his grandmother's face.

"Did he ride a horse?" Johnny asked.

"No, he walked, with only a small knapsack on his back, and he dressed in peasant's clothes so no one would recognize him. He didn't want people to try to impress a prince. He only wanted them to help a fellowman find the answers to life."

"So what happened?" Johnny murmured softly but urgently now.

Grandmother continued: "The prince went first to the largest town in his kingdom and searched until he found a grand house on a hill. It was an impressive home with four large pillars in front, and surrounded by lush lawns, flower gardens, and an ornamental reflecting pool.

"The servants ushered the prince into an ornate sitting room. A small round man, dressed in an elaborate brocade robe, rose to greet him. The prince had all he could do to keep from staring. The man wore jewels around his neck, on each finger, and on both ears, and a huge diamond hung from his nose. The prince thought him pretty gross!"

A small smile tugged at Johnny's mouth.

"'Sir, may I ask you two questions?' the prince asked.

"Flattered, the man said, 'Yes, yes, boy. Do.'

"'Please, sir, can you tell me what can bring happiness to one's years, and even more important, what is the meaning of life?'

"The man nodded and motioned for the prince to follow him to the rear of the house. There he pulled a huge key from his pocket and unlocked a massive door. The prince's eyes widened as he saw, inside the great storeroom, a mountain of gold and silver and chests of precious jewels—more wealth than he'd ever seen, even though he was a prince.

"The man laughed at the young man's expression and said, 'You should know that money will bring you happiness, and possessing it—and what it will buy—is what life is all about.'

"The prince frowned and shook his head slowly. The man *looked* happy enough certainly and yet . . . beneath the smiling exterior, the prince glimpsed a shadow. He turned away disappointed. *Was it true?* he thought. *Will money and possessions make me happy? And is acquiring them what one should do with his life?*

"Just as the prince was about to leave the storeroom, he remembered his mother's gift. On a whim, he reached into his knapsack, opened the box, and turned to look at the miser (for that is what he was) through the plain-looking, little piece of glass.

"Because of what he saw, he almost dropped the glass! The miser had disappeared, and in his place was . . . a *pile of dust!* The scene through the glass clouded a moment and refocused. The prince then saw the miser's children shrieking and fighting over the gold and jewels in the storeroom.

"Thoughtfully the prince left the lavish home. *No happiness there,* he thought, *and no purpose either. Only a pile of dust left of him and unloving children fighting for his riches.*

"Several days later the prince came upon a beautiful castle lived in by a man who, under the prince, ruled part of the kingdom. After several hours' wait, his audience with the ruler was granted.

"The prince bowed before the ruler (who did not recognize him) and said, 'Sir, I have two critical questions for you. What will bring one happiness, and what is the meaning of life?'

"The ruler, a tall man with a hooked nose, looked haughtily down at the prince, obviously feeling he was wasting valuable time.

"'Your question is too simple,' he intoned. 'Happiness is having power, and the purpose of life is to obtain that power so that you can have control.'

"The prince frowned. He knew *that* couldn't be the purpose of life because his father, the king, had had great power, and the prince knew he could inherit that power if he wished. Yet here he was on a search for true meaning.

"Just before he left the castle, he quickly took his magic glass and looked toward the ruler. He saw a man in prison, dressed in rags, hunched over and crippled. With sudden insight, the prince realized that in the future the power-hungry ruler would be overthrown because of his wickedness.

"*Power,* thought the prince, *is temporary at best, and control an illusion. Surely that road does not lead to happiness or the meaning of life.*

"After a few days of wandering, the prince walked into a small town with a great university. The beautiful ivy-covered buildings and spacious lawns provided a cool and restful setting for students to walk and discuss important issues of life. The prince inquired about the most illustrious and learned professor of the school and was directed to a quaint stone house in the middle of one of the college lawns.

"'Professor,' he began and stopped to look intently at the bearded, intelligent face. *Surely, this man will be able to help me with my search*, the prince thought. He continued, 'Professor, I need your help to find the answers to a great need in my life. Please, sir, can you tell me what is the way to happiness, and what is the meaning of life?'

"The professor rose, revealing that he wasn't as tall as he looked when sitting down. His vest bulged slightly over his stomach. Still he was an imposing figure as he came around in front of the desk and smiled benignly.

"'That is not an easy question, my son,' he said in his deep gravelly voice. 'In fact, it requires great study. But if you wish my opinion, I'd have to say that the way to happiness is found in learning, and the meaning of life—well, you will have to search further for that.'

"The prince sighed. If this man, who had studied all his life, did not know the meaning of life, who would?

"He turned away dejected. He didn't even want to look through the glass but decided that, if he was to be consistent, he should. So again, he took out his glass and looked toward the professor who once again was bent over his books. Through the glass he saw an old man in the same position, bent over a desk with books piled high, still searching but never having found the meaning of life.

"The prince shook his head sadly, thinking that perhaps there *was* no answer, no hope.

"As he left the town, he heard someone whistling. After rounding a great haystack, he saw a farmer, sweat glistening on his forehead, plowing with his mule.

"'Excuse me, sir.' The prince had to shout to be heard, but the farmer paused, wiped his brow, and said, 'What can I do for you, young fellow?'

"The strong red-faced man walked over to a deep well, lifted out a bucket of clear water, and proceeded to give the prince a drink and to take a long one for himself.

"The prince sat down on a bale of hay and without preamble said, 'Well, I need to know the secret of happiness and the meaning of life.'

"The farmer's laugh rang out over the hills. 'My boy, that's too much to think about for one so young. But if you ask me, happiness lies in work, and that's what life is.'

"'Does work really make you happy?' asked the prince.

"'Well, I don't really think about it much,' admitted the farmer. 'But I'm young and strong. And yes, I'd say I'm happy.'

"'But what happens when you get old?' inquired the prince.

"The man frowned and said gruffly, 'Why should I think about that now? No point in doing that.'

"'Well, thanks for the drink,' and with that the prince got up and said goodbye. He didn't even bother to look through his glass, because he knew he would see an old and helpless man with no future and no hope.

"A few days later, the prince came upon a huge circus tent, and from inside the tent came bellows of laughter. As he entered the tent, he saw a clown practicing his act before several children. Enjoying his performance, the prince waited until the clown was finished and then approached him.

"'Please, Mr. Clown, perhaps you can help me?' When the clown nodded, the prince told him about his search.

"'Well, your search is in vain,' said the clown glumly. 'I've tried it all. I've been everywhere and done everything, and it's all *nothing*. You know the saying, "Eat, drink, and be merry. . . ."'" His voice trailed off, and the prince finished it in his mind: '. . . for tomorrow you *die*.'

"The clown concluded, 'So you get what you can and laugh while you can, even if you don't feel happy, because there *is* no meaning in life.' He shrugged his shoulders, smiled wanly, and disappeared into a smaller tent.

"The prince turned away and ran into a nearby forest. He plunged deeper and deeper into the woods, not feeling the thorns and brambles that ripped at his clothing and skin. At last he fell to the ground and beat his fists into the hard earth. Then he screamed skyward, 'All right. All right. There *is* no meaning. There *is* no happiness. I might as well be dead!'

"For many days, the prince wandered through the forest, growing ragged and thin and wishing he could die.

"A long torrential rain drowned his last vestiges of hope, and utterly filthy and exhausted, the prince threw himself down by a rushing stream.

"But as he lay there, he became aware of the singing of a bird—the sweetest, most beautiful sound he had ever heard. *Why is that bird singing?* the prince wondered. *After all, it must have gotten drenched by the rain just as I did.*

"Suddenly his thoughts became clear and raced ahead. *Who made the bird to sing? Yes, who made the forest, the animals, and the rushing stream? Could it be . . . just could it be that the One who made the bird to sing would be the One who would know the meaning of life and happiness?*

"It was then he saw the rainbow! A perfect bow curved in the sky, and its end touched down on a nearby rock. Startled, the prince got up and stumbled over to the rock. The rainbow didn't disappear or move away from him.

"As he reached the rock, he saw an old man sitting on a large stone. He had a snow-white beard and hair, and he was bent from age and withered in body.

"The prince drew in a deep breath as he approached the figure and said, 'Sir. . . .'

"The old man looked up and smiled radiantly. 'Yes, my son, I've been waiting for you.'

Speechless, the prince sank down on the grass at his feet.

"'You have?'

"'Yes. But I had to wait until you had come to the end—not of your search, but of yourself. But now you are ready, and I will tell you the secret of happiness and the meaning of life.'

"The prince almost stopped breathing, so eager was he to hear the next words.

"'Your two questions are really one, my son. The secret of happiness and the meaning of life, of hope, of purpose can be summed up in one great truth. It is this: *knowing God*! for when you know Him, I mean really *know* Him, you have everything else. He made the birds, as you know, and the world around you— and He made you! But more than that, He loves you more than you can ever know. You will never understand His ways until you meet Him face to face. But as you know Him, your questions will fade as the joy of His presence is known to you.'

"The prince shut his eyes to let the old man's words sink in, and as he did so, a glow of happiness began to spread through his whole body. He never knew how the piece of glass got in his hand or why he held it up toward the crippled man; but as he did, he saw such an amazing sight that he dropped the glass, and it shattered against the rock. But then, he didn't care because he knew he wouldn't need it any longer. He had seen the old man—only he wasn't an old man any longer. As the prince looked into the future, he saw a young man clothed in brilliant white, strong and laughing, and somehow *eternal*. And the most amazing thing of all . . . the prince knew the old man was his father, the king!

"His father wasn't dead! His father was alive and strong.

"He looked up from the shattered glass and reached toward the old man. But the man had disappeared, and the rainbow was replaced by splashes of sunlight on the stream and rocks.

"The prince jumped to his feet with a shout of joy, and then leaped into the stream to wash the mud and dirt from his body, laughing with delight as he climbed from the water. He would go home. He would do the work he was meant to do.

"'Thank You, God,' he prayed. 'I will have joy as I know You. You give purpose and meaning to life—and even more than that, to death. Though why men give it such an ugly name, I do not know. For death is not death at all but an entrance into eternity.'"

There were tears on Johnny's face as his grandmother finished, and for a few minutes he sobbed quietly in her arms. Then he wiped his face with his sleeve, gave her a hug, and took her hand.

"Thanks, Grandma." He stood up and tugged a bit until she stood with him. His smile was genuine this time.

"Let's get Mom and go for a walk down by the river. Mom . . . well, Mom needs us to cheer her up, don't you think?"

Together, they walked into the house.

ABJECT FAILURE:
Losing Success

◆

My soul is in anguish.
How long, O LORD, how long?
(PSALM 6:3)

O bviously, the rental agent was in a hurry, but I was not about to be rushed. My heart stood on tiptoe as I gazed at the sprawling old house. We walked through an outside porch and entered a small hallway. To the left, a large living room with a high coved ceiling and a fireplace gave way to a smaller living room. This adjoined a gracious dining room, off of which was a comfortably sized kitchen and a sunny breakfast room—all set end to end, at least half a block in length. To the right of the entrance hall was a huge den, storage space, and half bath. Stairs led from the front hall to the upper level, where there were one small bedroom, two good-sized bedrooms, and one *huge* back bedroom, and two baths. Underneath the house was a full basement complete with washing facilities. A breezeway led to the small garage. Across the street was a peaceful park.

Inwardly I breathed, *O God, I need a miracle right now. We need the room, and the house is being offered at a ridiculously low rent—but three other people want it. Do You suppose, in Your kindness, that we could have it? It's just perfect.*

Outwardly I tried to appear nonchalant as I gazed around the house. I loved it! I didn't notice the cracks in the walls, the huge flowered wallpaper in most of the rooms, the dark kitchen. I didn't think about the fact that to get from the breakfast room to the front hall and upstairs to the back bedroom meant walking almost a block. We had been living in crowded conditions in a much smaller house in the middle of a motel complex. Four men and a couple lived with us as part of our ministry team, and I was ready for some ROOM.

When the agent told us we could have the house, I was ecstatic. One month later with a raft of helpers, we moved into that Victorian home. I sat among the unpacked boxes and sighed with relief and happiness.

That was the last time I felt relief and happiness for two years.

I guess I had thought a change of scenery would change the people we lived with and our relationships with them. But it didn't. Instead, negative situations worsened until they became monsters that haunted and destroyed.

That was the first time I can remember being stripped by God. Methodically. Deliberately. And Jack and I could not figure out what was going on. The stripping process caused deep and terrible anguish during the next months.

It began with one fellow who lived with us. Everyone liked cheery Henry. (I'm changing names, of course.) Henry always had a smile, remembered the latest jokes, and was quick to share what God was teaching him. He seemed open, responsive, teachable.

Sadly, Henry became the yeast that worked through the whole batch of dough (see 1 Corinthians 5:6). One day Henry confessed to Jack some ugly aspects about himself and his behavior over which he could not get control. Jack prayed about these matters with him and tried to help. But whether Henry was ashamed that he had told Jack his secret struggles, when later he still couldn't overcome them, or whether Jack didn't respond as Henry desired, we will never know on this earth. Suddenly Henry began to criticize Jack for things he thought Jack wasn't doing right. He told Jack and others what he didn't like about Jack, about me, about our home. Jack would apologize and try to make corrections, but nothing helped. We detected bitterness. And then the others in our home began to be poisoned too and became critical. The critical spirit spread to the ministry with college students until the ministry, so thriving before, was hurting, dying, and then dead.

We confronted Henry concerning his attitude, his backbiting, his bitterness, but to no avail. We were forced to ask Henry to move from our home, and he lied to others about the reasons. Because we could not break confidence concerning the circumstances he had confided, we were forced to remain silent when friends asked "Why?" One by one those nearest to us left our home and the ministry as well. We felt attacked on all sides and alone.

Then came the eviction notice in the mail. The old rambling house was to be torn down for a parking lot. No wonder it had been so reasonable to rent. We had no idea where to go.

The final heartache struck when friends I loved looked at me as though they didn't . . . love me. Or even like me.

I can still remember going to our room on one of many days and feeling not only destitute, but *not liked.*

On many days during this time, Jack told me that when he prayed, he felt as though the ceiling was made of brass and his prayers were bouncing back. As he read the Bible, it seemed that God was silent. Those were desperate days.

We had failed. Failed in helping people who were dear to us. Failed in the ministry God had put on our hearts. Failed in our desire to have people like us. Failed God. Failed people. Failed ourselves. Failed.

Everyday I would go to the Lord and say, "Lord, I know You have put us on the shelf for some reason. Maybe forever. But I don't know why. And God, I can't get through this day without feeling Your presence. Please—I *must have Your presence.*" And the Father would give grace for each day. Not for the following day but for that day. In that, I had to be content.

We had our health. We had our lively eight-year-old daughter, Lynn, who was a joy to our hearts. We had each other, and our love was never in doubt. No. This was a stripping of another kind. During those months we began to recognize it for what it was.

Until that time, we had never experienced failure. We were so sold on discipling people, so excited about the methods of doing that, so positive they were right and from God, that we didn't think we could fail. I guess my attitude was "With these principles—and a little help from God—we can't fail!"

And then we did fail. Miserably. Fell into the

mud with all our clothes on. Couldn't get up without falling again. And people stepped on us in the process.

I knew we couldn't expect to please everyone all the time. I even recognized that some people (Heaven forbid!) might not like me. But I grew up feeling, for the most part, liked. But now—ah, now—the only ones who seemed to like me were Jack and Lynn (and at really dark times I thought they did so only because they had to). My personality had failed me. I felt ugly, unattractive, and as though I had nothing to offer anyone. I grew depressed. My normally optimistic personality shriveled. I was

    . . . stripped of ministry.
    . . . stripped of the support of friends.
    . . . stripped of money.
    . . . stripped of personality and gifts.

During one particularly discouraging week, a godly man visited with us. Jack shared some of our struggles and told him of our failure. What he said has come back to me time and again. He said, "Jack, as I have studied men of God throughout history, I have come to the conclusion that every man worth his salt in God's Kingdom has experienced failure at some time in his life."

What an encouragement to us. We were not alone! If this were true, then God must *use* failure for some purpose in the lives of His children. Now our task was to find out what that purpose was.

Only in retrospect do most of life's lessons become clear. And so it was with this experience. But even as we were trying to see our way through failure, some truths were made known to us.

The first was the truth that we can count on nothing or no one for the ministry except God Himself. Oh, you say, who doesn't know that? Well, we *knew it*, we just weren't *believing it*. "Of course," we'd say, "this is God's ministry, not ours." But in our hearts the idea had somehow crept up on us that when these wonderful principles of discipling people were put into operation, the ministry would multiply no matter what. Of course, God would put His hand on it. Why wouldn't He? And so, subtly, without even realizing it, we were putting our trust in methods, in men, in tools. And God was demonstrating to us irrevocably that He alone does the work of the ministry.

The second truth, indistinct until afterward, eventually became a solid block for all time. It is spelled out in 2 Timothy 2:13 (NASB): "If we are faithless, He remains faithful; for He cannot deny Himself." Have you ever thought about this verse really? Paul seemed to switch structure in the middle of a paragraph. The two sentences before this one are conditional upon our actions: "If we endure, we shall also reign with Him; if we deny Him, He also will deny us" (verse 12, NASB). It stands to reason then that the next sentence should read, "If we are faithless, He will be faithless to us." But no! We read, "If we are faithless, He remains faithful." Why? Because *He cannot deny Himself*. God's very nature is faithful. He cannot be otherwise. To be so would be to deny Himself.

Am I ever glad for that truth, because during this time of failure, we felt faithless. I never doubted God's existence. I don't think I doubted His love. But I did doubt that He would ever use us again. I thought He had put us on the shelf forever, that He was through with us, that we had done something so irreparable,

He couldn't trust us as vessels of His love. I didn't know what that something was, but everything pointed to its existence. I knew I couldn't be separated from His love, but I thought I could be separated from some functions of that love. I doubted that we would ever be joyful again—or peaceful—or useful.

But after that time of stripping, God turned around and blessed us more abundantly than we could have imagined. He led us to a new place of expanded ministry and opened doors we could not have dreamed would be opened. He even healed broken relationships. In the intervening years, with the exception of that one man who, never allowing his bitterness to be healed, ended up lonely and divorced years later, every one of the relationships mentioned earlier was mended.

In the meantime, I fell in love with the Lord more deeply than ever before. Why? Because I saw His love when I knew I didn't deserve it, when I hadn't "earned" it. When I was down, discouraged, disheartened, and had given up internally, suddenly the floodgates of Heaven opened. In a mere month (after the pain and desolation of almost two years) God gave direction, people, ministry, joy, blessing—a 100-pound sack of His grace. As I wept in gratitude, I fell in love with Jesus all over again.

The third form to take shape in the gloom was the truth of God's work *in* us. In stripping away all the props of self, personality, and gifts, God made us realize the total nothingness of ourselves and the total everythingness of Him. We talk much these days about needing to feel good about ourselves. And when we see how much God loves us and cares for us, we can feel how worthwhile we are. But sometimes God wants us to know, feel, and understand that without

Him we can do *nothing* (see John 15:5). NO THING. I hope one lesson on this will be enough for Jack and me, because though vital, it was devastating.

God uses failure to soften us, because the hurt of defeat makes us sympathetic with the weaknesses of others. How can I be judgmental of others when I have failed myself? We must believe that God permits failure—that a loving God permits hard things; because the hard things bring the greatest victories, the deepest lessons, the most lasting changes.

Hannah Whitall Smith wrote in *The Christian's Secret of a Happy Life*:

> To the child of God, everything comes directly from their Father's hands, no matter who or what may have been the apparent agents. There are no "second causes" for them. Second causes must all be under the control of our Father, and not one of them can touch us except with His knowledge and by His permission.
>
> It may be the sin of man that originates the action, and therefore the thing itself cannot be said to be the will of God; but by the time it reaches us it has become God's will for us, and must be accepted as directly from His hands. No man or company of men, no power in earth or heaven, can touch that soul which is abiding in Christ, without first passing through His encircling presence, and receiving the seal of His permission. . . . Nothing can disturb or harm us, except He shall see that it is best for us, and shall stand aside to let it pass.[1]

You see, we are *successful* when we are steadily becoming the unique person God intends us to become and when we are doing what He asks us to do.[2] If this is an accurate definition of success, and I believe it is, then that success can and will at times include failure. One author says,

> Disappointments have forced me to wrestle with the truth that I can never fully figure God out and that I cannot put Him in a box. Hard times have made me realize I should not even pretend to know all His reasons for allowing me to go through what I go through. Frustrations cause me to trust Him even when I don't understand. Elusive success forces me to live by faith and not by sight.[3]

We only need a brief look around us to see that the world is full of hurting people. With so many tragedies, so much pain, such great rejection and in the midst of failure, how can we maintain joy?

A short time ago I concluded that being joyful depends on what I set my heart on and what I delight in. If I am delighting in relationships, they will disappoint me; in my husband and family, they may have to leave me; in job or money or possessions, they can be lost so easily; in reputation, position, or even ministry, these can be taken away or destroyed.

But a few *sure things* will *never* fail me, and if I delight in these, I will never be disappointed. I am to delight in the Lord, in His works, His Word, His name, His salvation, His world and mankind.[4]

You would have guessed those, wouldn't you? But here's the kicker! We are also to delight in *our own weakness*. You remember how Paul pled for the Lord to take away a "thorn in my flesh," but the Lord did not do it. Then in 2 Corinthians 12:9-10 he wrote,

But he said to me, "My grace is sufficient for you, for my power is made perfect in weakness." Therefore I will boast all the more gladly about my weaknesses, so that Christ's power may rest on me. That is why, for Christ's sake, I *delight* in weaknesses, in insults, in hardships, in persecutions, in difficulties. For when I am weak, then I am strong. (italics mine)

I've often said concerning speaking, "If I'm not scared, I get scared!" Now I know *why* I've said that. Should I then delight in fearfulness, in facing a situation too big or one I hate, in being afraid I might fall into temptation? Yes, I think so! Not so that I can give in to that temptation, that fear, but *so that* the power of Christ may rest upon me. Now *that* is big!

We are to delight in God but—wonder of wonders—*God delights in us!* Psalm 149:4 declares, "For the LORD takes *delight* in his people; he crowns the humble with salvation" (italics mine).

I am glad for the one who said, "No failure need be final." But in God's economy there is, sometimes, a final need for failure. When God uses the anguish of failure to strip us of all supports except Himself, we begin to grow up and to learn about the only sure truths in which our hearts can delight—to learn the absolute importance of sinking into God's love and allowing Him to be all there is.

NOTES:
1. Hannah Whitall Smith, *The Christian's Secret of a Happy Life* (Old Tappan, N.J.: Revell, 1952), pages 144-146.
2. Pamela Heim, *Push Me Gently, Lord* (Arlington Heights, Ill.: Harvest Publications, Division of Board of Educational Ministries, Baptist General Conference, 1985), page 122.
3. Smith, *The Christian's Secret of a Happy Life*, page 119.
4. See Nehemiah 1:11; Psalm 34:4-5, 35:9, 43:4, 111:2, 112:1; Proverbs 8:20.

CHAPTER 2

WAITING IN THE FOG:
Losing Sight

◆

How long, O LORD? Will you forget me forever?
How long will you hide your face from me?
How long must I wrestle with my thoughts
and every day have sorrow in my heart?
(PSALM 13:1-2)

e sat in the airport and sipped our coffee, feeling helpless. Airplanes nestled beside the building like chicks to their mother hen as the dense fog sealed us in.

Jack and I smiled grimly at each other and shrugged. The conference might have to begin without us, but there was absolutely nothing we could do. We couldn't go home, and we couldn't leave our city. We were immobilized.

An hour or so later, the fog suddenly lifted. We breathed a sigh of relief, a prayer of thanksgiving, and made it to that conference with only minutes to spare.

The fog of life is not so easily dispelled.

To me, fog is especially uncomfortable and, at

times, terrifying. I struggle with an impatient nature anyway, and to have my spirit fogged in gives me spiritual claustrophobia. I long to do something—anything—to dissipate the mist.

In truly dense fog there is nowhere to look—not up, down, front, back, or sideways. Spiritual fog likewise obliterates our view—upwards to God, downwards to Christ, the Rock beneath our feet; forward for direction and purpose; even backwards and sideways to what God *has done* in the past and *is doing* in the lives of others. As a result, we lose our sense of direction, our thankful spirit, and even sometimes our confidence and trust. We can't see God, feel God, or hear God. We are helpless and confused.

It seems to me that one characteristic of God's stripping action in our lives—whether through failure, fog, or other means—is our utter helplessness to do anything to stop it. And because we are people who like to be in control of our lives, the experience is excruciating. In other kinds of trials, we may have some control. If our neighbors are unbearable, we can move. If a friend hurts us, we can forgive and restore. If money troubles plague us, we can get a second job. However, the process of God's stripping puts us in a prison without doors. The prison of fog doesn't even have windows!

◆ ◆ ◆

I have always disliked *waiting*. My father drummed into his three children that we were late if we weren't five minutes early. Both my heritage and my impatient nature abhor waiting. Thus, when God puts me on hold, I begin to squirm. When He keeps me there, I fume, struggle, and strain. His patience with my impatience is incredible.

I am not talking about the times God says to wait while He works out a perfect way to say yes. Nor am I speaking of short-term delays. These are only wisps of fog swirling about the planes in the airport of our minds. But the dense fog of stripping is when all avenues of continuing are cancelled with no promise of future flights.

The first time God's fog drifted into our lives was a year after Jack graduated from seminary. We'd been enjoying that year, a year of firsts for us: first fulltime job in Christian ministry after seminary, first child (we didn't know then she was to be our *only* one), first year I hadn't worked outside our home. Then because of certain circumstances, God led Jack to resign his position as youth director. Another job opened immediately, but God wouldn't let us accept it.

It was then the fog settled in, in earnest. For four months, the three of us lived first with my folks and then with Jack's. Jack did everything from taking a government census of fruit trees to being a song leader for local evangelistic meetings. But no permanent job opened.

Each day I agonized and pleaded with God: "Please, Lord, open up the right job for us."

After two months of my begging, God began to deal with my heart. If He had spoken aloud, it couldn't have been clearer.

"Carole," He said accusingly, "you are anxious."

"Well, Father, I've certainly got something to be anxious about," I countered.

Then He reminded me, gently but firmly, of Philippians 4:6, which burned itself into my mind, "Do not be anxious about anything, but in everything, by prayer and petition, with thanksgiving, present your requests to God." *Do not be anxious . . . .*

I can still remember the tears of confession and my cry for help. I stopped praying for a job to open up and began to pray about the attitude of my anxious heart. In a miraculous way, God gave me peace during the next two months before He gave us the job of His choice.

Sometimes, in the fog of waiting, the lesson He will pound home to us is simply, *Do not be anxious.* Our own helplessness causes us to cry to Him to give us the strength and trust *not* to be anxious when everything within us screams with concern and apprehensiveness. Over and over He whispers, "Trust Me." It takes all our will—and great help from Him— to do just that.

What helps us when everything is obscured? When we seem to be marking time? When the fog closes in with vengeance?

It helps me to hang on to the knowledge that *even the fog is preparing me for Heaven.*

◆ ◆ ◆

I could hardly believe my ears! An evening for parents and prospective high school students was planned, and Lynn and I were listening to her counselor. He told the new students, "I have to be frank with you. When you apply to a college or university, all that will be looked at are your grades. So you need to get the best marks you can. Therefore, my advice to you is to take easy courses and get the best marks you can."

I thought I had mistaken his meaning. So afterward I asked him to clarify what he had said. "Sir, were you really saying that Lynn should take only easy courses in high school just so she can get good grades?" He acknowledged that this was what he had said.

"Then, sir, what happens when these students reach college and haven't learned to study, haven't learned the content of preparatory subjects, haven't been faced with the difficult courses?"

He looked a little sheepish but said, "Well, a lot of them flunk out. But that is the system."

As Jack, Lynn, and I talked about this advice, we felt it wasn't best to follow it. High school was, in Lynn's case, a preparation for college, and she needed the rigor of advanced courses to succeed.

If we see life as a training ground for Heaven, it takes on a new perspective. If, in God's training program, He schedules us for a life of failure in the eyes of the world, are we willing to live with that? If He designs times of confusion and thick mist, can we trust Him with that agenda?

Lynn was willing to live with some hard courses in high school because she saw the bigger picture. When we fix our eyes on Jesus, He helps us see . . . eternity.

Are we willing to stay put in the fog if God's plan is to use this to prepare us to *reign* with Him? Humanly speaking, I have to say no, but when I focus on Jesus, I can say yes. This foggy state may be incomprehensible to me now, but someday, looking down on planet Earth, I will say, "Oh, I see. You had to do it that way for me to learn. It really was the *best* way, wasn't it? But at the time I didn't understand."

In *Rose from Brier*, Amy Carmichael wrote,

"He shall choose our inheritance for us." I remember with what delight I found in *Young's Analytical Concordance* that the verb in this verse is the same as that used to show David's choosing, out of the possible stones in the

---

Your desire for my humility—
mist is part of the path.

knowing,
not understanding,
not seeing,
ols—important ones—
ching me . . . well,
as yet I know not what.

mist diffuses Your Light—
walls it back to me,
confuses the source of that Light.
able even to look down
o see the Rock beneath my feet.

only stand still
nd wait
nd listen
nd *hope*.

fog swirls in, my impatient nature is
ws. When the mist surrounds me, I
ow it away. My feeble attempts leave
ry, but I keep trying. Frustration
nthusiastic efforts end in deeper fog.
re to do is quit! Only God can lift the
does, I will see the way clearly.
ight the mist? It is God's breath!
e fog, I come to God looking for
ys to be content with weakness.
eking guidance. God fogs me with

"Now." God says, "Wait."
ard." God says, "Stay."

I come to God looking for answers. God shows me Himself.

I receive nothing that I ask for, but all that I need . . . to remain immobilized in the fog of indecision and waiting.

I whisper with David, "You hear, O LORD, the desire of the afflicted; you encourage them, and you listen to their cry" (Psalm 10:17).

Yes, even in the terrible confusion of the fog.

NOTE:
1. Amy Carmichael, *Rose from Brier* (Fort Washington, Pa.: Christian Literature Crusade, 1971), pages 176-1977.

ne five best for his purpose. So does our
David, our Beloved, choose out of all
circumstances (and they are all at His
d) the best for the fulfillment of His
1

one of His best "stones" is the fog,
the army of God behind us, the enemy
nt of us, or the triune God who is with

of years ago, I wrote:

n't like this!
Mist has fogged all certainty.
n't *see*!
re are no colors,
even black and white.
. . . gray.
No clear-cut outlines,
No vision of purpose
or plans.
cold, wet mist

terrified, lost, feeling abandoned.
within my heart I know that,
though I can't see You,
Your eye is on me.
Your hand holds mine . . .
even though its touch
is lost to me right now.

l from somewhere comes the
knowledge that in my
quest for humility—

CHAPTER 3

WHEN ALL PROPS GO:
Losing Support Systems

◆

Hear my cry, O God; listen to my prayer.
From the ends of the earth I call to you,
I call as my heart grows faint;
lead me to the rock that is higher than I.
(PSALM 61:1-2)

H e was perhaps fourteen, tall and a bit gawky—in that rather uncomfortable limbo of being not quite man, not quite boy. Dark hair. Large brown eyes. His mother herded him into the shop for a haircut as though he were some errant stallion, and for the next thirty minutes she cruelly and deliberately massacred him.

From the moment they walked through the door, her humiliating remarks were targeted with deadly accuracy. "Oh, I'm gonna kill that boy," she declared to the walls at large. Mostly she badgered him, "You've been horrible all day. . . . I can't take you. . . . How do I put up with you? . . ." Between jabs she ordered, "Sit up straight in the chair. . . . What's the matter with

47

you? . . . Sit up straight now, or I'll have them give you a Mohawk! . . . Sit up straight, I said. . . . Why do you make me holler at you? . . . No you can't have a pizza tonight. . . . After the way you've behaved, what do you think?" On and on she went. Once or twice the boy shot back at her, but most of the time he remained silent. Those of us in the shop winced with and for him.

I thought, *She's stripping him. Of all worth. Of all pride. Of all manhood. What a sad, sad thing for a mother to do.*

Aren't you glad that God never massacres or humiliates or belittles? He does what needs to be done in our lives with love. Oh, to us it doesn't always seems that way. But our God is strong, loving, and consistent.

However, there are times when God lays us bare, depriving us of every prop we lean on, divesting us of anything in which we might take pride, stripping us until there is nothing left to strip away. The process is never done in cruelty or anger, but it is deliberate and thorough and many times leaves us numb at best, or doubting His love and interest in us at worst. This kind of suffering often brings *doubt* to our lives.

Jack and I have been through the process of stripping, and we have observed as close friends have gone through it too.

◆ ◆ ◆

It was eight o'clock one cloudy night when the doorbell of our townhome in a Chicago suburb rang urgently. We were startled to find Dave standing there looking disheveled and wild-eyed.

"Dave!" Jack exclaimed. "Come on in. What are you doing here?"

Dave brushed past Jack and, looking anxiously about, pleaded in a low desperate voice, "I had to see you. But I think I'm being followed. They've been tracking me everywhere. You and Warren are the only people I can trust. They almost got me in a store where I stopped while driving here. You've got to help me."

In less than two minutes, we knew that Dave was a very sick man. It had taken him nine hours to make what should have been a three-hour drive from his home to ours. He was convinced the Communists were taking over the country, and Jack and one other man he trusted had to be notified. Dave was also convinced those enemies would try to kill Jack.

The only thing that calmed Dave was reading the Word of God to him. Jack soothed him as best he could and finally got him to try to sleep on the hideaway bed in the office. As quickly as we could, we called a friend who was a psychiatrist for advice. We told him we would need to bring Dave in to see him the next morning. He warned us that a person that ill could harm those he cared about if, in his deluded state, he felt they, too, had turned against him. We woke Lynn, then a preteen, and told her to lock her bedroom door. She was so sleepy she complied without question and went back to sleep. I was grateful she didn't experience our terror.

When all was quiet, I called Dave's wife, Jane, certain she would be frantic about Dave's mental state and where he was. But as I talked to her, I realized she had no idea of his illness. Yes, he had told her the police and others were out to get him. Yes, he had been taken to the police station for odd behavior. Yes, he had become increasingly fearful and critical in the last weeks. But he was a wonderful husband and had never lied to her. *She believed everything he told her.*

When our furnace clicked on early the next morning, Dave thought "they" had set fire to the house. He tried to get all of us to run for our lives as he ran screaming out the door with nothing on but his pajama bottoms. We had to call for help then, of course, and Dave was admitted to the ward for mentally ill patients at a nearby hospital.

His wife stayed with us for the next several weeks. During that time I saw a dear friend stripped methodically of every one of her supports. She could no longer look to her husband for help. He was frantically trying everything from cajoling to threatening to make her get him out of the hospital. Her own parents were unable to help her emotionally, and her in-laws actually blamed her for Dave's illness. Her small children were bewildered. Dave didn't have insurance, and the medical bills piled higher every day. All the props for Jane's life were taken from her one by one until she was humiliated, destitute, and despairing.

I wanted to help. I assured her she wasn't at fault. The one thing she might have done was to have become aware of Dave's illness before it got to the point of hospitalization. She had made the mistake of keeping her eyes on her husband instead of on God, and in her eyes Dave could do no wrong. She submitted to his judgment completely and trusted everything he did and said.

Nothing wrong with that, is there? Well, yes, there can be. When a husband or a wife *is not more sensitive to God* than to his or her spouse, trouble can develop because then we fail to admonish one another, to call each other to account, or to help one another when our perspective is maimed.

But because God had led us through a stripping

process of another kind the year before, I realized we humans should not and must not undo what God is deliberately doing. We can encourage and support. But we must be careful not to try to negate His working.

Oswald Chambers admonished,

> The saint who satisfies the heart of Jesus will make other saints strong and mature for God. The people who do us good are never those who sympathize with us, they always hinder, because sympathy enervates.[1]

Realizing I might undo what God was teaching Jane, I tried to be careful not to over-sympathize.

After Jane's soul was shorn of all human support, after her weeks of heartache and pain, God began to rebuild her life—both of their lives really. Dave and Jane determined to get out of debt within a year, and they worked hard, cutting out all nonessentials, to do so. A little at a time, Jane blossomed forth with new and growing branches on the stripped vine of her soul until, once again, she thrived and bloomed.

You may ask, "Is it *God* who does this?"

Psalm 66:10-12 was brought to my attention not long ago. It reads: "For you, O God, tested us; you refined us like silver. You brought us into prison and laid burdens on our backs. You let men ride over our heads; we went through fire and water, but you brought us to a place of abundance."

"You let men ride over our heads." Interesting phrase, isn't it? I've felt that. People were "riding over my head," crushing me, hurting me, being cruel. And where was God? I couldn't see Him. I couldn't feel Him. And yes, I doubted Him! Yet He was there all the time. And when He finished the excruciating process, He lovingly gathered all the broken pieces and put me back together again as a different person. I'm grateful for His faithfulness.

Occasionally our supports are taken from us gently, one by one, as God undergirds us with His strength. But mostly the buttresses bracing the bridges of our lives collapse simultaneously or so quickly we are left defenseless and gasping.

Often we are unaware of our dependence on these supports until they fail us. We've talked about failing, we've discussed the spiritual fog; but the supports I refer to now are sometimes not thought of as underpinnings until they crumple beneath us. I'm talking about community, friends, organizations, a financial base, children, and even a marriage partner.

Not too many years ago, God began to teach Jack and me some mighty lessons concerning the props we had been leaning on without even realizing it. We went through a period when people we had thought of as friends turned out not to be; when those we counted on were not there; when security seemed as slippery as a lotioned back; when we looked around, and no one seemed to be there for us.

At one time Jack thought even I didn't understand what he was going through. (Fortunately, that didn't last long, but it gave us both a taste of what it must be like for someone to feel that a marriage partner's understanding has evaporated.)

It was then that God began to pound into our lives the truth of Psalm 62:1: "My soul finds rest in God *alone*. . . . He *alone* is my rock and my salvation; he is my fortress, I will never be shaken. . . . Find rest, O my soul, in God *alone*; my hope comes from him" (verses 1-2,5; italics mine).

Jack spent days studying and meditating on the truths of this psalm, and God's Word helped and sustained him through that period.

How often, subconsciously, we add to verse one. We say, "My soul finds rest in God . . . and in an understanding wife or husband, in good health, in financial security, in people who appreciate me, in a fulfilling work situation." On and on we go. Oh, not out loud. But if you look at how we *act*, then it would be common knowledge that our expectations are in a number of things and people. Yet the psalmist cries, "God *alone*."

And why? How can this be?

The answer is found in the last verses of Psalm 62: "One thing God has spoken, two things have I heard: that you, O God, are strong, and that you, O Lord, are loving" (verses 11-12).

Isn't that something? God speaks one thing. The psalmist hears two. Why? Perhaps because from man's viewpoint, being strong and being loving are two characteristics of the character of God. But from God's viewpoint, they are so intertwined, they become one.

And what are they? He is strong and therefore *able* to help us with the problems of our lives. He is loving and therefore *willing* to help us with the problems of our lives.

Isn't that terrific?

Whenever something seems to hit me below the belt and totally knock the wind from me, I am learning to examine my heart to find out if the reason for my disappointment and pain is that I have begun to have expectations in something or someone other than God. Oh, of course, people can hurt me. What kind of stoic would I be if nothing or no one could faze me?

But if I am *devastated* by situations and people, perhaps a "checkup" by Psalm 62 is needed.

A little phrase tucked into John's gospel merits great consideration. In talking about some people who believed in Christ but refused to acknowledge and really follow Him, the writer said, "For they loved praise from men more than praise from God" (John 12:43).

I've been challenged to "fill in the blank" here. "They loved _____ more than praise from God." A love affair? Money? Comfort? Success in the eyes of the world? The popular decision?

What do I love, what do you love, *more* than *praise* from God?

Until we know in our hearts, minds, and souls that we want *nothing* more than praise from God, we will rant and storm and protest when "men ride over our heads"; when people, organizations, and friends don't meet our expectations or desires; when our world seems to be collapsing and our support systems fail.

But *if* (and that's a mighty big *if*) our hope and expectations are really in God alone, we can rest secure in His willingness and ability to be all that we need.

Hey, friend! Have any men ridden over *your* head lately?

NOTE:
1. Oswald Chambers, *My Utmost for His Highest* (New York: Dodd, Mead & Company, 1935), page 223.

CHAPTER 4

INEXPLICABLE INCAPACITATION:
Losing Strength

◆

Be merciful to me, O LORD, for I am in distress;
my eyes grow weak with sorrow,
my soul and my body with grief.
My life is consumed by anguish and my years by groaning;
my strength fails because of my affliction,
and my bones grow weak.
(PSALM 31:9)

He came to our wedding in the back of a pickup truck, his wheelchair held steady by two friends. We welcomed him with joy, happy he had made the heroic effort to attend.

Only a few black families lived in Three Rivers, Michigan, where I grew up, and my mother had befriended them all. But Rev. Blackwell was exceptional. A crippling disease had invaded his body twenty-five years before and had crept upwards from his feet, paralyzing each part it touched.

I remember vividly the times I visited him with Mother. His shriveled body was imprisoned in the wheelchair, his useless hands in his lap. His wife had to care for all his functions, including feeding him.

But his face! Ah, his face! It was as though he was illuminated from the inside. His broad and genuine smile lit up a room. Even as a young teenager, I recognized something unique and wonderful about him. To visit him was a pleasure and inspiration rather than a duty, because when you were in his presence you knew you were with one who had a singular relationship with God. God's Spirit permeated the room where Rev. Blackwell sat.

After my parents moved from Three Rivers, I lost touch with Rev. Blackwell. But I will never forget him.

I greatly admire those saints of God who have been chosen to bear inexplicable incapacitations that last for the better part of their life span. I have observed only a few who bore their long-term disability and pain with patience, courage, and surrender. Most of us ordinary human beings find constant pain and illness difficult, if not impossible, to accept gracefully, let alone to accept it as from God. Most of us *despair*. But those persons who do accept it—and eventually embrace it as Rev. Blackwell did—*shine*.

We all either know personally or know about such people. We read the works of Amy Carmichael who spent many years unable to walk. Yet she ran her mission, wrote extensively, and helped multitudes in India all from the prison of her bedroom. We are inspired as we read the books by Margaret Clarkson and Joni Eareckson Tada. We think as we read them, *I don't know if I could be so brave if I were continually in pain, ill health, or a quadriplegic.*

But although I've never met either Margaret or Joni, I am sure they would tell me they do not have extraordinary courage nor are they any other than "ordinary" human beings.

No. It isn't that they are extraordinary as people.

Rather they have determined to put their trust in an extraordinary God. Did you get that? The key word is *determined*.

The determination of the psalmists strikes me again and again. Psalm 73 exemplifies both the writer's despair and his steadfastness.

Actually much of this psalm sounds just like me on a bad day! The psalmist was really letting it all hang out. He was complaining. He was having a party to feel sorry for himself with no one invited but God. To paraphrase a bit, he was saying, "Goodness gracious, Lord, those arrogant so-and-so's are having a ball. They are healthy, wealthy, and proud of it."

Can't you just see this man with the back of his hand on his forehead saying weakly, "They [the wicked] have no struggles; their bodies are healthy and strong. They are free from the burdens common to man; they are not plagued by human ills" (verses 4-5). To sum it up, Lord, they are "always carefree" (verse 12).

Then he turned from how well off the wicked are to how unfortunate he was. "All day long I have been plagued; I have been punished every morning" (verse 14). He concluded the first harangue by saying that even trying to *understand* what he was going through was oppressive (verse 16), that is, until he entered the sanctuary of God; then he understood (verse 17).

Determination. The resolve on the psalmist's part to do what he knows will help—go to God.

He then reflected on his self-pity and admitted, "When my heart was grieved and my spirit embittered [notice he admitted to bitterness during this time], I was senseless and ignorant; I was a brute beast before you" (verses 21-22).

His determination rose again. "Yet I am always

with you; you hold me by my right hand. You guide me with your counsel, and afterward you will take me into glory" (verses 23-24).

In a final great crescendo of praise and decision, he declared, "My flesh and my heart may fail, but God is the strength of my heart and my portion forever" (verse 26). God is. The psalmist declared God to be, determined Him to be, willed Him to be his strength and portion forever.

One recent morning I got up tired—well, I have to admit it—I was more than tired. I was empty, depleted, used up. For over two months Jack and I had been away from home every weekend and sometimes during the week. I was weary of travel, fed up with plane delays, exhausted from pressures and people. I looked at my day, and the day stared back at me with a vengeance. A dozen Mickey-Mouse but necessary errands loomed large. Driving back from one of those errands, struggling to keep going, I took a good look at myself and realized my condition. The tyranny of the urgent had robbed me of the important—once again.

Many times I grit my teeth and keep going, but this time I *determined* to do what I should have done several days before. I shelved the tyrannical pressing errands, took my Bible, went into a small upstairs room, and closed the door. Somehow God led me to Psalm 51, a rather plaintive psalm really, but it contained just what I needed in verses 10 and 12. "Create in me a pure heart, O God, and renew a steadfast spirit within me. . . . Restore to me the joy of your salvation and grant me a willing spirit, to sustain me." I prayed David's prayer, and God answered in an abundant way. Out of nothing He created. He renewed. He restored. And He granted. I came away filled up with Him.

I kept returning to those verses the next week, and suddenly the phrase "grant me a willing spirit, to *sustain* me" slapped me on the shoulder. I would have said, "Grant me a willing spirit to keep me going, or to make me obedient." David said "to sustain me."

Why?

Suddenly I had a mental picture. The young mother had a firm, determined grip on her small boy's hand as they came toward me. Good thing! Because with all his might, the boy tugged back and dug in his heels in a fruitless effort to resist her leading. The unwilling little boy expended at least three times the energy (as did his mother) as he would have if he had walked beside her *willingly*.

Ever tried to drive a car with the emergency brake on? What a hassle! The forward motion is hindered greatly. But when the brake is released, the momentum is *sustained.*

A willing spirit *sustains* our momentum and our freedom to obey God joyfully, without reserve.

I think the indescribable burden of constant pain and illness takes a special kind of courage and determination, a willing spirit that *sustains.* The ability to determine to praise God and trust Him in the months and years that the illness or disability continues doesn't just happen. And I am talking about *years*—or perhaps a lifetime, as was the case with Rev. Blackwell.

I've never been through that kind of stripping, but I have observed others who have been. I have been in enough pain for shorter periods to know it is difficult—extremely difficult in some cases—to pray, to listen to God, to concentrate on His Word, even to think. So I know it must take special grace and great effort for a person to rise above his circumstances instead of sinking beneath the waves of pain, incapacity, and illness. But I also know God's grace exists. He has said that when more grace is needed, more grace will abound . . . that *nothing* is too hard for Him . . . that He can and will give us victory.

I can still remember seeing Joni on closed-circuit television from a basement of a church in which she was speaking. (We arrived too late to sit in the auditorium itself.) As she sat helpless in her wheelchair, she told us that when she was first paralyzed, she prayed for a complete healing. She wanted to be part of the first "heroes of the faith" in Hebrews, chapter eleven. She wanted to be among those who were raised from the dead, healed of diseases—those to whom God granted a miracle. But as time went on, she realized God might keep her among the heroes in the last part of the chapter—those who were not delivered, those who were torn apart. Yet God saw them all as "heroes of faith." She told us that one Greek word for "power" is *dunamis* from which we derive the words *dynamite* and *dynamo*. She wanted the "dynamite" kind of power, a blast of power that would heal her body. But she knew God was giving the "dynamo" kind of power that would sustain her day by day.

Then came the words I will never forget. With the sweetest smile, she said, "And if you don't think it takes dynamo power from God to continue to sit in this wheelchair and smile, you are mistaken."

A person who lives day after day, month after month, year after year with disability and pain needs God's dynamo power. It is there, but each one has to avail himself or herself of it.

As I have observed the Rev. Blackwells of my life—Christians living in the power and grace of God—I think they have discovered a secret most of us are unaware of. Oswald Chambers called it the "baffling call of God" and quoted Luke 18:31,34: "And all things that are written by the prophets concerning the Son of Man shall be accomplished. . . . And they understood none of these things."

Chambers elaborated:

God called Jesus Christ to what seemed unmiti- gated disaster. Jesus Christ called His disciples to see Him put to death; He led every one of them to the place where their hearts were broken. Jesus Christ's life was an absolute fail- ure from every standpoint but God's. But what seemed failure from man's standpoint was a tremendous triumph from God's, because God's purpose is never man's purpose.

There comes the baffling call of God in our lives also. The call of God can never be stated explicitly [*explicit* means characterized by full clear expression—unreserved and unambigu- ous in expression]; it is implicit [meaning sug- gested or to be understood though not plainly expressed—implied]. The call of God is like the call of the sea, no one hears it but the one who has the nature of the sea in him. It cannot be stated definitely what the call of God is to, because His call is to be in comradeship with Himself for His own purposes, and the test is to believe that God knows what He is after. The things that happen do not happen by chance, they happen entirely in the decree of God. God is working out His purposes.

If we are in communion with God and recognize that He is taking us into His pur- poses, we shall no longer try to find out what

His purposes are. As we go on in the Christian life it gets simpler, because we are less inclined to say—Now why did God allow this and that? Behind the whole thing lies the compelling of God. "There's a divinity that shapes our ends." A Christian is one who trusts the wits and the wisdom of God, and not his own wits. If we have a purpose of our own, it destroys the simplicity and the leisureliness which ought to characterize the children of God.[1]

God's call to us is often baffling. What God calls "good" looks anything but good from our point of view. Who could call years of pain and seeming uselessness "good"?

But when God's call looks baffling to us, that is the time we must *determine* to trust Him . . . to call on His grace to be sufficient for us.

The stripping from pain and helplessness is, in the hands of God, a tool of consequence and one not used indiscriminately. He does not trust the majority of us with this kind of life. Many of those He does call are crushed by the stampede of constant pain, weakness, and incapacitation. But those who come forth in victory—ah, those are the ones whose faith has been tried as gold. They come through the fire shining, their faith burnished, glowing, and pure.

Had an extra-special room been prepared for him when God said, "Welcome home, child" to Rev. Blackwell?

I'm sure of it.

NOTE:
1. Oswald Chambers, *My Utmost for His Highest* (New York: Dodd, Mead & Company, 1935), page 218.

CHAPTER 5

CHARACTER ASSASSINATION:
Losing Self

◆

For I hear the slander of many;
there is terror on every side;
they conspire against me.
(PSALM 31:13)

T hey sat across the table from us at a nearby restaurant. Even before our lunch was served, we asked them, "What has happened to you?" and they shared their sad ordeal.

He was a respected Christian statesman, an authority on reaching a whole section of the world for Christ, and God led him to start an organization to facilitate doing that. For several years he enjoyed success and prestige.

Then his world crumbled. Through perfidy and slander, his reputation was damaged. The board of the organization he had founded asked him to resign. He and his wife were left broken, emotionally battered and torn.

As we talked over lunch, his wife glanced sideways at her gentle-faced husband and confessed, "He's taking it well, but I'm angry and bitter."

I couldn't blame her. I've nearly been there myself.

◆ ◆ ◆

I bit my lip and tried to hold back the tears to no avail. I got up off my knees and reached for my notebook and wrote:

> Do You know how I feel, Lord?
> > Do You?
> I feel like Jeremiah did *before*.
> > Before You lifted him out.
> I'm in a slimy pit.
> > Mud.
> > Mire.
> I claw at the walls.
> > Scratch.
> > Scream.
> My fingernails bleed
> > from the attempt
> > to climb from the pit.
> I slide back down
> > into the muck.
> > I'm stuck!
> My every attempt
> > meets
> > with failure.
>
> I'm trying
> > to hang on
> > to Your promises.
> In my heart I know
> > there's a Rock
> > beneath my feet.

Please, God,
    may my heart's knowledge
    of that Rock
And the reality of *feeling*
    that Rock
    become one and the same.
Soon.

My desperate cry was not because the cloth of my life had been torn by physical pain, the death of a loved one, or desperate circumstances. I cried because several strands of character assassination had been handstitched into my life at the same time.

Character assassination. Even the phrase makes me cringe.

All of us have had people say unkind and malicious remarks behind our backs and even to our faces. Those hurt. Sometimes terribly.

But character assassination is in a different category. It can be a machete in the hands of God, whacking at the tree of our lives with deep and devastating strokes.

Assassination is (1) "to murder by surprise attack" or (2) "to harm or ruin as by slander, vilification."

Character, in the sense used here, is "essential quality; nature; kind or sort; or reputation."

Character assassination then is the deliberate, surprising murder of a reputation, and with this kind of stripping often comes the awful feeling of *rejection*. Few of us over a lifetime are immune.

Jonathan Edwards was the leading theologian and minister in New England in the 1700s. He and his wife, Sarah, enjoyed a prestigious and successful ministry in Northampton, Massachusetts, for a number of years. Then something happened. Criticism concerning their lifestyle and handling of finances started ugly little fires among the townspeople. In the spring of 1750,

> townspeople shunned the Edwards family, refusing to talk with them on the street. Church attendance was only a fraction of what it used to be. A petition was circulated and 200 church members signed it asking for Edwards' dismissal as minister. By mid-year Jonathan was unemployed.[1]

Sarah and Jonathan ended up in Stockbridge, Massachusetts, living in a log cabin surrounded by wigwams. "He preached in a small stuffy room through an interpreter to a small congregation, mostly of Indians who had covered themselves in bear grease as a protection against the winter cold."[2]

Several years later Rev. Edwards accepted an offer to be president of the school that later became Princeton. But before Sarah could sell the house and join him, he was stricken with smallpox and died. Shortly afterwards, Sarah also died.

Recently, I've been thinking about Joseph of the Genesis story, who was accused by his boss's wife of trying to rape her. He was thrown into prison and forgotten! Few men in the Bible are portrayed without fault. Except for possible pride as a boy, we find no flaw in Joseph. Did you ever wonder why? Could it be that in the several processes of God's stripping in Joseph's life, God had really purified this servant? Joseph was stripped of

> . . . support of family, home, and comfort when he was sold into slavery.

. . . his reputation when Potiphar's wife falsely
accused him.

. . . his freedom when he was jailed unjustly.

To maim someone's character is a heinous sin.
But we aren't considering the person who has done
the deed, we are looking at the person it is done to. If
we really believe nothing can touch us except what
has gone through the hand of God, then this too is
allowed of Him. Therefore the lessons in it are from
His hand. Oh that we could view the world and our
situations from His point of view!

A friend of mine wrote the following:

Our plane had been circling the Denver airport
for thirty minutes. Tired and frustrated, I kept
staring at the thick cloud cover that was
responsible for our delay. As the plane turned, I
was startled to see the most beautiful oranges,
yellows, and pinks brilliantly scrolled across the
sky. Tears sprang to my eyes. I guess that I had
never witnessed a sunset from 30,000 feet! I
was so deeply moved by this bold reminder
from God that the following thought resulted:

Etched into the sunset,
the signature of God.
In radiant script
He signs
I AM.[3]

From God's point of view, even the cesspool of a
reputation ruined can have His signature on it. He
really is signing "I AM," even as we are squirming and
wriggling to extract ourselves.

In those years of exile, Jonathan Edwards did some serious writing. His most famous piece of philosophical writing, *On the Freedom of the Will*, was written in Stockbridge. The legacy we have from this man comes mostly from those years when God was signing His "I AM" in a special way across his life.

Joseph's life was signed clearly when he said to his brothers, "You intended to harm me, but God intended it for good" (Genesis 50:20).

Our friends, the Christian statesman and his wife, look back and see God's sign over their damaged lives.

And we do too.

◆ ◆ ◆

What are we to do when people around us seem bent on assassinating our reputation? Well, when the church at Northampton couldn't find another minister to fill Edward's shoes, he filled the pulpit of the church that had boisterously evicted him. He preached without bitterness, as Sarah and her daughters made lacework and embroidery and painted fans, which they sent to market in Boston to help make ends meet. No wonder God used that family in unique ways. No wonder that a study of 1400 descendants of Jonathan and Sarah Edwards revealed a legacy of "13 college presidents, 65 professors, 100 lawyers, 30 judges, 66 physicians, and 80 holders of public office, including 3 senators, 3 governors, and a vice president of the United States."[4]

What did Christ do when Judas betrayed Him?

I read the words with wonder.

He called him "friend"!

In the very act of betrayal, Christ called His betrayer "friend." (See Matthew 26:50.)

Shortly before, Jesus had told Judas what He knew Judas was about to do.

Shortly after, the betrayer committed suicide, knowing he had betrayed not only the Son of God, not only a companion of over three years, but also one who, even as Judas's lips touched His cheek, looked at him steadily and called him "friend."

Amazing, *agape* love. Love that reaches out in the face of greed, bitterness, envy, hate. Love that beams steadily no matter the character of its recipient. An active, passionate love.

◆ ◆ ◆

Christ is our ultimate example of one who was stripped.

He was literally stripped of everything, emotionally, spiritually, and physically.

They tore away His clothes and left Him naked before a taunting mob.

His friends either turned on Him, denied Him, or ran away.

Three of those closest to Him didn't stay awake to pray with Him even though He told them He was in great emotional need. They went to sleep. He begged them to support Him in prayer. They went to sleep again. This time He let them sleep. Perhaps even in His deepest anguish of heart, His compassion for their physical needs surfaced above His own need. Perhaps He thought they'd need the sleep to face what was ahead. So He prayed alone.

He had no home, no possessions, and even His clothes were taken from Him and used for gambling.

He was shorn of His dignity, His position, His support, His reputation.

In the final horror, He who had never sinned,

became sin, and in doing so His Father had to turn His back on His Son. In terrible agony of soul the Son cried, "My God, my God, why have you forsaken me?" (Matthew 27:46).

The Lord Jesus suffered the terrible humiliation and pain willingly because He loved us with an all-compassionate love.

But, we argue, it was the only way for Christ to atone for man's sin. He *had* to do it. But why should we suffer unjustly?

Perhaps the best reason is because He commands it!

Peter made a thought-provoking statement in the context of telling us what we are to do when we suffer unjustly. He said,

> Slaves, submit yourselves to your masters with all respect, not only to those who are good and considerate, but also to those who are harsh. For it is commendable if a man bears up under the pain of unjust suffering because he is conscious of God. But how is it to your credit if you receive a beating for doing wrong and endure it? But if you suffer for doing good and you endure it, this is commendable before God. To this you were called, because Christ suffered for you, leaving you an example, that you should follow in his steps. (1 Peter 2:18-21)

As I read verse 19, "It is commendable if a man bears up under the pain of unjust suffering because he is conscious of God," I wondered exactly what it was about God that made a person willing to bear *unjust* suffering. As I reflected, I realized that one would have to believe in the complete *love* and the complete *sovereignty* of God in order not to step in and stop that unjust suffering—that is, if you could do something about it at all.

At times, Christ stepped in when the suffering of others was at stake, but at other times He didn't. He fed the five thousand when they were hungry, for instance, but He didn't do anything about John the Baptist when he was in prison and then beheaded. He delivered both Peter and Paul from prison but allowed Paul to be shipwrecked, beaten, and taken to a Roman prison. Christ didn't do anything about His *own* suffering, although He certainly could have. He is God! Instead, He allowed Himself to be beaten, spit upon, mocked, and finally crucified.

I am not sure what the implications of Christ's actions are for us. Surely there must be times when we should step into a situation to stop a vicious lie; to clarify what has been misinterpreted or misrepresented; to defend a position or reputation. Yet two of the most godly men I know chose never to defend themselves even against monstrous lies concerning them. Maybe we fight back too soon to allow God to do His work. In the light of Peter's words, would it seem to you that perhaps we need a clear word from God to *step in* rather than a clear word to *stay out* of the situation? To defend ourselves might be to miss the truth of 1 Peter 2:19: "For it is commendable if a man bears up under the pain of unjust suffering *because he is conscious of God*" (italics mine).

When we are being mistreated, when we are being stripped of reputation and personality, we *must* hang on to the fact that, as Jean Fleming writes in *Between Walden and the Whirlwind*, God is not only the Director of our lives but also our *Audience*.[5]

❖ ❖ ❖

The actor had given his all in the performance that night, and at the conclusion the audience rose to its feet and clapped fervently—all except one heckler who had crashed the gate. In a loud voice, he yelled, boo'd, and whistled derisively until an usher came to eject him from the hall.

The next evening the heckler picketed the play, but no one paid him heed. The actor was bothered, but managed to put the incidents from his mind.

After the evening's performance, the prompter, who positions himself just in front of the orchestra pit, drew the actor aside and told him softly that he had blown an important line. The actor made a note to himself, thanked the prompter, and assured him that he would correct it in the next performance.

If it is true—and it is—that God is both the Director of our lives and the Audience, what do we do with hecklers and prompters?

If we get confused and begin to believe that the hecklers *are* the audience, we are in real trouble. But if we don't pay attention to the prompter (one who is *part* of God's team for us), we are also in trouble.

Most of us encounter any number of hecklers during our life's performance, and we should ignore them. We are blessed also with some prompters, to whom we must pay close attention. But above all, as we play out life's drama, our all-consuming thought should be the fact that God is directing every moment, and it is He who observes and either smiles or shakes His head in sorrow at our performance.

What is the Director's purpose in the events of our lives? Well, one of His purposes is to make us into the kind of vessels He wants us to be.

My mother-in-law sent me this lovely poem recently:

The Vessel

The Master was searching for a vessel to use.
Before Him were many, which one would He
    choose?

"Take me," cried the gold one. "I'm shiny and
    bright,
I'm of great value and I do things just right.
My beauty and luster will outshine the rest.
And for someone like you, Master, gold would
    be best."

The Master passed on with no word at all.
And looked at a silver urn, grand and tall.
"I'll serve you, dear Master, I'll pour out your
    wine.
I'll be on your table whenever you dine.
My lines are so graceful, my carving so true.
And silver will always complement you."

Unheeding, the Master passed on to the brass,
Wide-mouthed and shallow and polished like
    glass.
"Here, here!" cried the vessel, "I know I will do,
Place me on your table for all men to view."

"Look at me," called the goblet of crystal so
    clear,
"My transparency shows my contents so dear.
Though fragile am I, I will serve you with pride,
And I'm sure I'll be happy in your house to
    abide."

Then the Master came next to a vessel of wood,

Polished and carved, it solidly stood.
"You may use me, dearest Master," the wooden
　　bowl said.
"But I'd rather you used me for fruit, not for
　　bread."

Then the Master looked down and saw a vessel
　　of clay.
Empty and broken it helplessly lay.
No hope had the vessel that the Master might
　　choose,
To cleanse, and make whole, to fill and to use.

"Ah! Now this is the vessel I've been hoping to
　　find.
I'll mend it and use it and make it all mine.
I need not the vessel with pride of itself,
Nor one that is narrow to sit on the shelf,
Nor one that is big-mouthed and shallow and
　　loud,
Nor one that displays his contents so proud,
Nor the one who thinks he can do things just
　　right.
But this plain earthly vessel filled with power
　　and might."

Then gently He lifted the vessel of clay,
Mended and cleansed it and filled it that day:
Spoke to it kindly—"There's work you must
　　do . . .
Just pour out to others as I pour into you."[6]
　　　　　　　　　　　　　　　—B.V. CORNWALL

　　I'm coming to believe we must *expect* the kind of
stripping in our lives that makes us know we are only

vessels of clay. For many of us that means a stripping of reputation. Few escape a time when reputation is lost to some degree. There are few who don't *need* what it accomplishes. The refining fire of the loss of reputation burns away the dross in our lives and purifies us perhaps in a way nothing else can.

If it happens, may we not stand bewildered. May we face it head on with Christ as our example. May we respond to this humiliation and rejection in a way that people will see God's signature upon our lives. For He *will* sign "I AM."

NOTES:
1. William J. Peterson, *Martin Luther Had a Wife* (Wheaton, Ill.: Tyndale House, 1985), page 94.
2. Peterson, *Martin Luther Had a Wife*, page 95.
3. Cynthia Heald, *The Creator, My Confidant* (Colorado Springs, Colo.: Nav-Press, 1987), page 83.
4. Peterson, *Martin Luther Had a Wife*, page 75.
5. Jean Fleming, *Between Walden and the Whirlwind* (Colorado Springs, Colo.: NavPress, 1985), pages 21-35.
6. Source unknown.

CHAPTER 6

ALONENESS:
Losing Intimacy

◆

I am forgotten by them as though I were dead;
I have become like broken pottery.
(PSALM 31:12)

Look to my right and see;
no one is concerned for me.
I have no refuge;
no one cares for my life.
(PSALM 142:4)

hat are we having for breakfast, Mom?"

I stared at Lynn blankly for a long moment, waiting for the silt of confusion to settle. Instead, mounting waves of disorientation swirled relentlessly and, with increasing fury, muddied the waters of my mind. Suddenly a dark thought focused and broke to the surface in conscious frustration: *Why* was Lynn asking such a difficult question?

In that moment I realized I was in trouble.

The extremely busy summer had culminated with two weddings just two weeks apart. Both brides were dear friends who had been living with us, and because their parents lived in other parts of the country, I was up to my eyeballs in the wedding plans. That was fun but stressful.

I have often said that if a wedding doesn't have something go wrong, the couple will not be properly married. If that is true, the last couple who married that summer will be married for eternity. Everything went wrong! The dress for the maid-of-honor never arrived, and at the last minute the bride's mother was frantically trying to find and fit another dress. On the night of the rehearsal, a hurricane-like storm hit Chicago. As we were driving to the rehearsal, a garbage can careened from an alley and struck our car—hard. With great difficulty, we drove through deeply flooded streets to the rehearsal dinner held at a lovely restaurant on the shores of Lake Michigan.

When we returned home, we saw the full extent of the storm. Arriving to a completely dark house, we suspected the power had been off for some time. Realizing the sump pump couldn't work with the electricity off, we took a flashlight to investigate the lower level of our house. Carefully we inched down the stairs and, at the bottom, stepped into five inches of water. Not only was Jack's office on that level, but all the bride's gifts were down there and many boxes stored for the groom. Fortunately, the gifts were all on tables except a pillow in a plastic bag, which floated! Nevertheless, it was a mess.

Also that night, we looked in vain by flashlight for a pair of rented shoes for one of the ushers. (We never did find them and later realized that the rental agency failed to include one pair.)

The power stayed off through most of the next day, and I couldn't prepare the "after wedding" supper I had planned for our guests.

We made it through the wedding—which turned

out to be lovely in spite of everything—and a friend invited us and our guests to her home for supper. I got home from the wedding, looked at the catastrophe in the basement, started to change clothes to go to our friend's house, and began to cry. I couldn't stop. Jack had to excuse us from the supper, and after crying for hours, I finally fell into an exhausted sleep.

It was the next morning that Lynn asked what we were having for breakfast and I found myself staring at her in mounting confusion. I felt as though I were coming apart. It was as if I were two people: one bewildered at what was happening; the other detached, uncaring, seeming to view the situation from a long distance away.

Somehow we got through the next two days, while some men who had been in the wedding helped us clean out the basement. Then Jack took Lynn and me to Wisconsin, where for several days I did nothing but rest, sit by a lake, and sleep. Those few days—along with withdrawing from some of my former activities and responsibilities for a period of time—enabled me to recover. I have realized since that experience that I was close to a physical and emotional collapse, which God enabled us to catch before I slipped over the edge.

Most of us experience such times to some degree. I can remember vividly an incident when Jack was close to collapse. He preached on the importance of memorizing Scripture in a church one Sunday morning, but he couldn't remember a single verse of Scripture himself! Fortunately, we recognized that as a sign of stress and took measures immediately.

It seems when God writes some episodes in the book of our lives, He declares "Cease and desist!" just before the event actually lays us bare. Although these near misses often come in the same forms as true stripping times, they do not hold the same degree of intensity.

But the line is a fine one when events cause isolation and aloneness. God may be the only one who can discern if an event is near-stripping or the actual tearing away of supports to the degree of stripping itself.

There are probably different technical definitions for the terms *emotional exhaustion, nervous breakdown,* and *emotional collapse.* But whatever the term and to whatever degree the illness, whether one is close to collapse or over the edge, one facet of the difficulty is emotional distance—an alienation from others—an aloneness that is difficult to define.

Symptoms vary of course. Loss of motivation, increasing irritability, a wiped-out sense of humor, deep tiredness, diminished capacity for work, fuzziness of thinking—all can be part of the problem that results in the feeling of aloneness, the wondering if *anybody* understands or cares.

◆ ◆ ◆

The kitchen was spotless, but she kept wiping the countertop with a damp blue sponge. "I've been stripped," she confided. "And it hurts so much. It's a result of not having a relationship with my own daughters. I have friends who are closer to me than my family. I'd give anything if my daughters and I were close." She continued to rewipe the counter with the sponge.

Hard to believe, I thought. *She's so dear, so dedicated, so godly,* and I gazed at this petite wife and mother who gives seminars, leads a large Bible study, and has a beautiful friendship with her husband.

How little we can know from outward appearances. Most people would never dream that behind my friend's sweet face and gentle smile is a grieving heart—caused by the failure of relationships she longs to have. This woman had reached out to her married daughters in every way she knew how. They had taken the gifts, the loans, her time, and her help but had rejected her friendship, her love, her *self*. Over the years, continual episodes of rejection pricked open the initial wound, leaving a gaping hole in her very personhood. That illustrates one small aspect of the emotional loneliness of rejection. There is also the terrible inward isolation that comes when we feel there are few who know us, who "watch out for my soul" (Hebrews 13:17, KJV).

◆ ◆ ◆

I lie on my bed and stare at the ceiling. I cannot sleep. My body is tired, but my mind is racing one hundred miles per second. My thoughts are troubled as I think about the events of the evening.

We were out with a couple for dinner. It was a good dinner. A nice time. But, oh, so superficial. We asked polite questions, and they responded with polite answers. They didn't ask questions of us, so we shared little about ourselves.

Typical, I think. *Like so many other evenings. Pleasant but inane. Neither of us knows—really knows—the other, and apparently that's sufficient.*

Then my heart winces with a thought.

How many people do I know who really do know me, who care what is going on in my life? Who take the time to listen? Who are vulnerable to trust me with their thoughts and feelings and who they are?

I look toward Heaven and breathe, "You do!"

I turn in the darkness and look at my husband sleeping peacefully by my side. I smile as I whisper softly, "You do!"

"Then there's Lynn and Tim . . . they care. And there's. . . ." I pause. Thinking of our few close friends, I stop to thank God for each one.

My mind turns more slowly now and is suddenly ground to a halt as a thought sharply strikes a mental cog. *How many in this world . . . ?* My eyes open widely with the thought. *How many people have no one at all who really understands? No human. Some don't even have You, Lord. No wonder so many are desperate, despondent, depressed.*

I force myself to stop thinking.

I sleep.

◆ ◆ ◆

We hear much talk in Christian circles these days about our need for a support or accountability group and for various kinds of people to be "on our team." I couldn't agree more. But for most of us, we plan to work on that "next month," or we wait for someone else to organize such a group, or we're afraid of rejection should we say to someone, "I would like to have you as a caring friend."

The self-help books on the subject say we should seek out several kinds of people to hold us accountable, to be on our team, but they don't tell us how to do that. So if we try at all, we creep up on it so tentatively that people may not even see our movement toward them.

I wonder what would happen (would the sky fall on us, or the earth drop beneath us?) if we said to that hoped-for friend, "Whom do you have you can talk with, who supports you, whom you can count on? Do you feel the need for someone like that? Might I be a person like that for you? Would you be willing to give some time to see if real friendship might develop between us?"

Of course this is only part of the human solution to aloneness, a solution that is temporary at best and disappointing at worst, because God wants us to know that our needs are met in Him *alone*. However, there are times when God very well *may* meet our needs through someone with skin on.

Aloneness may be due to the very real fact of physical separation from those we love. When we are physically separated, obviously mental and emotional separation is part of the package. Goodbyes hurt. And we have all said our share of goodbyes.

I must admit, tears clogged my throat when we received a letter from our daughter, Lynn. It was written from Mexico, where they live, to those close friends and relatives who pray for her and her family. A poignant letter, it started:

> LONELY: 1. alone; solitary
>   2. standing apart from others of its kind
>   3. unhappy at being alone; longing for friends, company, etc.
>   4. causing a feeling

> Their bags were all packed, the plane was about to take off, and we were aching our way through yet another good-by. Wonderful memories were fresh in our minds—the carpet croquet game, the shopping, the long trek through our town, the late-night heart-to-heart talks, the laughing, the experiences. The sweet-

ness of the memories made the good-by especially hard . . . again!

Loneliness has been on our minds recently. For some reason, this last month our hearts have been more tender toward "homesickness." We've missed the fall trees turning color, a hamburger from McDonalds, keeping up with the Chicago Bears, and getting to see our new-born niece. It has not been a continual throb, but rather an occasional, unexpected prod; tapped by a memory, an incident, a word or a song. Would you, those whom we know really care about us, PRAY that these moments of nostalgia would not be sad, but rather sweet, that they would place in our hearts not bitterness, but deep gratitude for all God has given. And pray for others too whom you know that are far away. Pray hard.

Lynn enclosed a quote from Max Lucado in his special book *No Wonder They Call Him the Savior*, in which he says:

In fact, it seems that goodbye is a word all too prevalent in the Christian's vocabulary. Missionaries know it well. Those who send them know it, too. The doctor who leaves the city to work in the jungle hospital has said it. So has the Bible translator who lives far from home. Those who feed the hungry, those who teach the lost, those who help the poor all know the word goodbye.

Airports. Luggage. Embraces. Taillight. "Wave to grandma." Tears. Bus terminals. Ship docks. "Goodbye, Daddy." Tight throats. Ticket counters. Misty eyes. "Write me!"

Question: What kind of God would put people through such agony? What kind of God would give you families and then ask you to leave them? What kind of God would give you friends and then ask you to say goodbye?

Answer: A God who knows that the deepest love is built not on passion and romance but on a common mission and sacrifice.

Answer: A God who knows that we are only pilgrims and that eternity is so close that any "Goodbye" is in reality a "See you tomorrow."

Answer: A God who did it himself.

"Woman, behold your son."

John fastened his arm around Mary a little tighter. Jesus was asking him to be the son that a mother needs and that in some ways he never was.

Jesus looked at Mary. His ache was from a pain far greater than that of the nails and thorns. In their silent glance they again shared a secret. And he said goodbye.[1]

Is there any lonelier word than *goodbye*? The goodbye of death, of divorce, of separation, of children leaving home, of parents forced into a nursing home? My heart aches with goodbyes. And it bubbles when I remember that one of the glorious joys of Heaven is that there will be no goodbyes. That fact in itself makes me want to shout hallelujah!

But while most goodbyes bring the pain of both physical and emotional distance, they can't be compared to the heartache of seeing the mental deterioration of someone we love. Often we feel the ache of a final goodbye as they leave us to go to a place where we cannot follow. The internal and psychological distress of that kind of emotional distance is the worst kind of goodbye. When we watch a loved one suffer the humiliation and terror of an emotional or mental breakdown, a part of us is mortally wounded.

I saw it happen to my mother, and I hurt just remembering it.

Mother turned a deaf ear to death's whisper when a large tumor and tubal pregnancy caused unparalleled havoc in her body. When she was in her early forties, the doctors prescribed all kinds of pills to help her back from the precipice, pills that were addictive.

That was the start of the years of decline. I saw my vital, talented, full-of-life mother become, in some ways, the antithesis of all she had been. At first, Daddy tried to shield us children from what was happening. But after my father died of leukemia, Mom had to enter a sanitarium, which was a nice word, in this case, for a mental hospital. She was there for three years. She had not only lost her husband but also her freedom and her ability to write and to minister to groups. Mother lost her capacity to think clearly, to remember well, and to choose the people with whom she lived. It was terrible for her. But it was also terrible for me.

To see her change . . . to see a person who abhorred a lie become a liar . . . to see a writer and speaker, wife and mother living confined, incapable of relating well to the outside world . . . to see an open, up-beat woman become suspicious and furtive . . . oh, that was hard.

During those years I lost the woman I knew as mother.

Many times I cried out to God to heal her or take her Home. But He didn't. There was some progress. She was able to leave the hospital after three years and live in a tiny apartment, then in a retirement home. Her optimistic personality returned and with it her desire to help people. But Mother was never to "be there" for me again.

Alone. Even the word looks cold and bleak. It makes us hunch our shoulders against the cold; droop in weariness and despair; shrink from the blasts of seemingly senseless tragedies we face every day of our lives. It makes us want to retreat from life itself.

At least it would if we left it there.

But we can't leave it there anymore than the men who wrote the psalms could leave their laments and complaints without a further word. Anymore than Jeremiah could weep without turning his face toward Heaven. And yes, anymore than the Lord Jesus could have been left in the grave.

We are reminded of something so full of wonder that it brings our eyes from the ground of our hopelessness to a sky streaked with color and light.

For the truth is there for all of us to grasp even in darkest despair: Aloneness and isolation are impossible for a Christian. *We can never be isolated*—we are never alone—because God is always with us. Whether we feel Him or not. Whether we recognize His presence or not. *He is there.* He has said, "So do not fear, for I am with you; do not be dismayed, for I am your God. I will strengthen you and help you; I will uphold you with my righteous right hand" (Isaiah 41:10).

So let's reach out to Him and ask to *feel* His presence, to *experience* His friendship, and to be supported by His strength.

The secret of surviving the stripping of isolation is realizing that, for the Christian, isolation is impossible because

God is with me.
God is in me.
God is.
God.

I need to sink into His presence. Let Him surround me with His glow. Snuggle into His arms. Bury my face in His lap. Rest.

I must picture myself as that little lamb wrapped in the arms of the Shepherd, carried by Him, protected by Him, befriended by Him. I must keep His face before me; make Him the focal point of my thoughts and mind until I *do* feel Him.

In my aloneness, I'm never really alone.

I am never isolated. I am never apart from God.

My great Shepherd has declared, "*Never will I leave you; never will I forsake you*" (Hebrews 13:5).

I wonder why I fear? What can *man* do to me when the living God of the universe is with me, within me, delights in me, is *for* me?

My heart shouts with David: "Therefore my heart is glad and my tongue rejoices; my body also will rest secure. . . . The LORD lives! Praise be to my Rock! Exalted be God my Savior!" (Psalm 16:9, 18:46).

NOTE:
1. Max Lucado, *No Wonder They Call Him the Savior* (Portland: Multnomah, 1986), page 41.

CHAPTER 7

IN THE VALLEY OF THE SHADOW:
Losing Loved Ones

◆

O God, have pity, for I am trusting you!
I will hide beneath the shadow of your wings
until this storm is past.
(PSALM 57:1, TLB)

At 4:00 a.m. Saturday, November 21, 1987, I awoke when suddenly Jack flung his arm across my shoulders. I sat bolt upright and asked, "What's wrong?"

Even in the dim light, I could see his face grimaced in agony as he replied, "I think I'm having a heart attack."

I rushed to the phone and dialed 911. A calm voice intoned, "What is the nature of your emergency?"

"I think my husband is having a heart attack."

"What is your address, please?"

I staccatoed the address to her.

"Are you in the same room as your husband?"

"No."

"Will the phone reach him?"

"No."

She then began to ask questions I thought were ridiculous in the light of what was happening. Finally I burst forth, "Look, my husband needs an *ambulance*. Please hurry!"

Calmly she replied, "Paramedics and the fire department are on the way right now. Don't hang up the phone but go unlock the door, put any pets away, and then come back to the phone."

I ran and opened the door, turned the alarm system off, grabbed a robe and slippers, and had just picked up the phone again when I saw the flashing red lights outside our house. Both paramedics and firemen had responded within five minutes of my call.

They took charge quickly, carrying Jack downstairs on a chair before putting him on a stretcher. I followed the ambulance to the hospital two blocks away after slipping slacks and a blouse on over my pajamas, reaching the hospital just as they did (I drove faster!).

By this time, the sharp pain in Jack's chest and shoulder and down his arm had gone, receding even before the nitroglycerin and oxygen had been administered. Jack was feeling a bit sheepish over the whole episode, but the doctor wasn't so sure it was a false alarm. He insisted Jack be kept for observation for a day and a half to monitor his heart and take further tests. How grateful we were when the blood tests, EKG, and even a stress test Monday morning came back negative. Later, it was determined a large gallstone was the culprit.

After leaving Jack in the hospital that evening, I contemplated the hectic events of the day and wondered why the Lord often chooses to let the greatest shocks and losses in our lives (death of spouses, children, friends) happen at a time when we are less able physically to handle them. In other words, as we get older and more infirm, we have to handle some of the greatest pains and difficulties life offers. I realize that is not true for everyone, but with most of us it is. As the Lord and I were talking it over, He reminded me of the truth of 2 Corinthians 12:9: "But he said to me, 'My grace is sufficient for you, for my power is made perfect in weakness.' Therefore I will boast all the more gladly about my weaknesses, so that Christ's power may rest on me." The truth of that verse will *shine* in situations where I feel especially weak, for *His strength* is made *perfect* in my weakness. Therefore I need not fear.

"And besides," He added as He whispered to my heart, "what makes you think infirmity of the body is also infirmity of the soul?"

I realized then that as we learn to trust God through the years, let's hope our souls will stretch and grow and learn to rest in Him to the degree that we can handle the deep valleys better in the winter of our lives than when we were younger. There are other reasons, no doubt, for the deepest sorrows to be laid on older shoulders. But one thing is sure: I can trust Him with my life and with my death—and Jack's, though that will be harder.

When James Means lost his wife to cancer, he wrote a heart-searching book called *A Tearful Celebration*. In it he says,

> A precious life has been taken away. I feel great grief and pain. It sears my every waking hour.
> At a time like this, it is imperative that I remember that God has not promised to keep my life bubbling with good, pleasing sensa-

tions. I must not prostitute God by giving Him the responsibility of being an indulgent Santa Claus in the heavens. God is not my servant. I am His servant.

. . . God's comfort is not insulation from difficulty; it is spiritual fortification sufficient to enable me to stand firm, undefeated in the fiery trials of life. God's provision is not always the green pastures and still waters. Sometimes God leads into the valley of the shadow, but I may walk there with confidence.[1]

Grief shatters. It shatters comfort and happiness. It consumes our strength and our energy. We become preoccupied with it, focused on it, drained by it. It shatters our world and the people in it. And in most cases, grief is something from which there is no escape.

If you haven't faced it yet, you no doubt will, my friend. A beloved parent, a sister or brother, a close relative, a dear friend. Grief that grabs you in massive jaws and seems to tear you into ragged pieces.

One of the greatest hurts in life surely comes from losing a marriage partner.

I wish I knew who handed me this heartrending cry:

WHAT IT'S LIKE TO BE YOUR WIDOW

It's being devastated by the seemingly simple act of discarding your toothbrush . . .

It's sorting through your clothing: wrapping the empty sleeves of a sportcoat around me and sobbing into its lifeless shoulders . . .

It's realizing too late the pettiness of complaining about shoes left in the living room at night . . . wishing we'd talked more . . . regretting that I hadn't been more tender and weeping because there's no opportunity to make it up to you.

It's returning to familiar or favorite places that first time without you and feeling so alone . . .

It's missing the lingering smell of your shaving lotion after a good-bye kiss . . .

It's eating alone at the counter of a restaurant on Easter Sunday because no one remembered that I was alone . . .

It's losing my champion and cheerleader . . .

It's having to depend on an electric blanket for warmth on cold wintery nights . . .

It's sitting alone in church and at weddings and being especially touched by "'til death do us part" . . .

It's knowing your only daughter will not walk the aisle to meet her bridegroom on your arm and our joy will be terribly marred by your absence . . .

It's struggling to keep my composure at seeing your empty place at the dinner table especially on your birthday, our anniversary and holidays . . .

It's knowing your first grandchild is on the way and will never climb into your lap and experience that special love you had for little ones . . .

It's not finding comforting arms when I rush home hurt and bruised by a conflict . . .

It's keeping your robe because it's the last piece of normal clothing you were able to wear . . .

It's trying to see through tears driving home from work as I remember you won't be there . . .

It's not hearing, "Honey, I love you" or "You really look good in that dress" . . .

It's wondering if you know how very much you're loved and missed . . .

But it's also knowing that even if you could come back, you wouldn't—not after being with the Lord Jesus Christ. Nor could I ask you to trade the company of the Altogether Lovely One for that of a very imperfect wife but, oh, how I do miss you![2]

Widows often face more than the consuming loss of their husbands. Many face the loss of financial support, friendships, ties with people from their husband's profession, business counsel, and the loss of the thousand little things he took care of without her even being conscious of it.

If Jack dies before I do, I'll lose my organizer, the

one who sees to the cars being serviced, the yard mowed, the snow shoveled, repairs done around the house. I will lose the keeper of the records, the financial manager, my advisor, and trip organizer. All that *besides* the horrifying loss of comforter, supporter, friend, lover, companion.

If strong supports are in place—the support of children, friends, financial security, for instance— then the loss of a marriage partner, while being a painful and deep valley to walk through, may not necessarily be used by God to show us that our soul finds rest in God alone. But my guess is that, for the most part, losing a life partner even in the best of circumstances, financially and with support systems in place, is used by God to forge deep lessons in our lives.

◆ ◆ ◆

Pat's warm greeting and bright smile welcomed me as I made my way down the steps of the small commuter plane. We climbed into her car and began the drive to the church for a women's retreat.

I learned much from Pat that weekend as I stayed in a small apartment beneath her suburban house. I discovered that even when a husband leaves a wife financially secure, when she has dear supportive children, when she is busy and working for the Lord, even then the pain of widowhood is excruciating and debilitating.

Pat's forty-nine-year-old husband lived only eight painful weeks after cancer had been discovered. Her children, church, and friends stood with her. But after her husband had been laid to rest and the carefully-prepared covered dishes from friends had been eaten, the grief descended with vengeance—

and most people around her did not know how to help her. She inwardly cried for friends to understand, to listen, to pray, to share the Word, to call. But few did. She felt alone, bereft, confused.

God has used these three years to mold Pat and use her in unique ways. She's involved in a hospice program, she shares with young marrieds, she is sensitive in unusual ways to those hurting around her. More than once that weekend, I saw her with arms around a hurting person, talking quietly.

And she challenged me. Pat spoke of being given the "*gift*" of widowhood." I have never heard that term before. The *gift* of widowhood! She said the death process should be similar to the birth process. There is pain in both, but there should be *joy* in both as well—the *joy of passage*. Birth passing to physical life, death to eternal life.

I looked at her in amazement. In my heart, I questioned whether her attitude was real. But after talking deeply with her that weekend, I was convinced she believed with all her heart what she said.

Pat probably got her analogy from Christ when He warned His own disciples about their coming grief, followed by joy, in His death and resurrection. He said, "You will grieve, but your grief will turn to joy. A woman giving birth to a child has pain because her time has come; but when her baby is born she forgets the anguish because of her joy that a child is born into the world. So with you" (John 16:20-22).

It takes most of us years to get past the pain of such a loss and look for the reasons for that pain. James Means says,

> I have observed that God sometimes deems it
> necessary to remove from me the external signs

of His blessing in order that the pressure of darkness might prompt me to a new level of trust in Him. In God's reckoning, to descend is the path to ascent, to suffer is to find freedom from suffering, to taste darkness is to approach eternal light, to become weak is to become strong. Each agonizing moment is essential or God would not allow it. To be counted worthy of suffering is to enter an entirely new realm of spiritual experience. My suffering is seen as instrumental, not accidental, to the purpose of a loving God.[3]

Pat's darkness has prompted within her a new level of trust, a new realm of spiritual experience. No wonder she called it a gift!

The devastation of grief—this kind of stripping—is characterized by prolonged and overwhelming *pain*, a pain so intense that it terrifies. One reaction to this kind of anguish may be to grit our teeth, refuse to give thought to the sorrow, and grow hard in our spirits.

Jack and I sat talking to a couple who were hurting deeply. Their only son and heir had been killed in a frightful farm accident two years before, just after graduating with honors from high school. He had earned scholarships to a prestigious university and was on the brink of a wonderful life when suddenly, inexplicably, his life abrubtly ended.

Tragic.

What was even more heartbreaking was what that loss was doing to this couple's marriage. The wife desperately needed her husband's comfort and support. She needed him to listen to her and talk about their son's death with her.

But he wouldn't. From his viewpoint, he couldn't.

He had bottled up his grief, pressed on a pain-resistant cap, and then sealed it under layers of determination. But he had paid a terrible price for his repression, because all his other emotions had gotten trapped in that bottle as well. He appeared cold, uncaring, and distant both to his friends and to his wife. No one could get in to help him, and he couldn't or wouldn't climb out of his self-imposed prison. Repression was choking his emotional life little by little.

The gulf widened between him and his wife.

I shared with that couple the vivid memory of a time during my sister's suffering with leukemic meningitis. Her brain had swollen within her skull, causing her excruciating pain. To watch her suffering was almost more than I could bear. So when I was away from her, I refused to let myself think about it. Of course thoughts came unbidden but, as quickly as they surfaced, I stomped them under.

I was afraid. Afraid I'd lose control and not be able to stop crying. Afraid of the state in which a crying jag would leave me. Actually afraid to *trust God with my pain*. Then I saw the title of a little book called *Don't Waste Your Sorrows*, and it dawned on me that I could very well be doing just that.

So one day I went into my little study room, closed the door, got a box of tissues ready, sat down and said to the Lord, "O.K. Father. I'm going to sit here, review the horrible, painful times, pray, listen, and just *hurt*. Teach me all You need to in this hurt because I don't want to waste my sorrows."

For some hours I cried, remembered, prayed, wept, and poured out my grief, frustration, anger, disappointment, and lack of comprehension. My heart felt as though it would shatter into a hundred pieces. But when I rose from my knees, I felt great release . . . as though I had been cleansed, comforted, relieved. Strange. Instead of destruction came restoration.

Some considerations may be appropriate.

First of all, and especially for those of us with overly active imaginations, night is *not* the time to allow our thoughts free reign. When we are tired, our imaginations grow even more vivid, things look darker, situations worse. We must discover the truth of the line in Shakespeare's *Macbeth*: "Sleep that knits up the raveled sleeve of care." Things *do* look better in daylight.

Second, it may be wise to limit our whys as we talk to the Lord. Oh, we will have them. And God understands. Even the Lord Jesus asked why on the cross when He said, "Why have You forsaken Me?" But too many whys is a dead-end street. God holds the missing pieces of our lives safely in His loving hands, and *we must leave them there*.

Finally, don't bottle up tears. God holds your tears in *His* bottle, so *you* don't have to bottle them up within you.

Picture yourself held securely in the arms of the Shepherd. Or paint a mental picture of Heaven with all the details, and then underneath your picture write: *This is nothing compared to the real thing!* Or think about the birth process resulting in physical life and the death process passing to eternity. Sing a song about Heaven softly to yourself.

Devastating grief is one of God's shaping tools that most of us would not choose. But the choice is not ours.

Amy Carmichael wrote:

THE QUARRY

His thoughts said, The time of preparation for service is longer than I had imagined it would be, and this kind of preparation is difficult to understand.

His Father said, "Think of the quarry whence came the stone for My house in Jerusalem."

THE TOOLS

His thoughts said, I wonder why these special tools are used?

His Father said, "The house, when it was in building, was built of stone made ready before it was brought thither; so that there was neither hammer or axe nor any tool of iron heard in the house, while it was in building.

"If thou knewest the disappointment it is to the builders when the stone cannot be used for the house, because it was not made ready before it was brought thither, if thou knewest My purpose for thee, thou wouldest welcome any tool if only it prepared thee quietly and perfectly to fit into thy place in the house."[4]

My human tendency is to want to reject the ordeal of deep and prolonged grief. But friends, let's pray that each of us may be willing to accept *any* tool in the Master's hand that will mold us and shape us into His image.

As we pray, may we, each one of us, be able to look with spiritual eyes into Christ's face, to see His compassion and love, and to rest in His care. Only then will we be assured that not one of our devastating sorrows will be wasted in the school of our lives. Only then will we be comforted as we feel the blanket of His love wrapped around us when He whispers, "Precious in the sight of the LORD is the death of his saints" (Psalm 116:15).

> The son asked, What is death?
> His Saviour answered, I will come again and receive you unto Myself; that where I am there ye may be also.
> The son repeated those peaceful words, I will receive you unto Myself. . . . And he wondered that men had given so harsh a name to anything so gentle as that which those words signified. They seemed melodious to him, each word like the pure note of a bell. And they were, he thought, as full of life as a flower in the sunshine is full of light.[5]

NOTES:
1. James E. Means, *A Tearful Celebration* (Portland: Multnomah, 1985), page 19.
2. Author and source unknown.
3. Means, *A Tearful Celebration*, page 38.
4. Amy Carmichael, *His Thoughts Said . . . His Father Said* (Fort Washington, Pa.: Christian Literature Crusade, n.d.), page 1.
5. Carmichael, *His Thoughts Said . . . His Father Said*, page 122.

CHAPTER 8

THE COMING OF WINTER:
Losing Youth

◆

Do not cast me away when I am old;
do not forsake me when my strength is gone.
(PSALM 71:9)

T he aspen are turning in Colorado. Shades of gold brush across the deep green mountain, looking like an ethereal Renoir painting. In the distance, snow-capped peaks thrust jagged edges into woolly clouds.

The frost last night killed the masses of petunias but left the pansies and geraniums to brave another cold snap. I revel in the beauty.

Yet, it is a nostalgic time, knowing that soon the hills will be stripped bare of the aspen gold, the pines shrouded with white, the flowers gone.

Only once in our lives have we lived in a place without seasons, a place somehow trapped in perpetual summer. For me, it was a love-hate relationship. I rejoiced in not fighting the icy streets, shoveling snow, cleaning off windshields. But I missed the newness of spring, the fullness of summer, the colors of autumn, and yes even the snows of winter.

We often speak of old age as the winter of our lives, but in my opinion winter comes to us at many ages. It comes when the golden leaves of joy have fallen, leaving our hearts bereft and brown; when grief chills our hearts; and when unfulfilled dreams and lost hope strip the color from our days.

Each passing decade is traumatic for many. A friend of mine who just turned forty wrote, "I HATE getting older." And I could empathize.

I smiled as I read recently:

I'll grow old, I suppose—
(It's the better choice.)
I'll accept it, though scarcely
A cause to rejoice.

But this you should know,
And I'm going to shout it;
DON'T EXPECT ME
TO BE GRACEFUL ABOUT IT![1]

Forty was a crisis birthday for me. It was a time for reflection; for consideration of where I'd been and where I wanted to go in the years ahead; of clarifying goals; of realizing that if I got off course one degree at forty, by the time I was sixty, I would be so far off track I'd miss the goal completely. It was a time to pray, evaluate, and consider.

Reading Isobel Kuhn's *Ascent to the Tribes* was sobering that month. When the Communists gained control, Isobel and her husband had to flee China and their beloved Lisu people with whom they had spent many years. They settled in Dallas and loved it. When they were asked to go to Tibet, Isobel faced having to learn a difficult language and living in a frightening land among a hostile people. She didn't want to go. Then, as she read Scripture, she noted that "at the time when kings go off to war," David *stayed home* (2 Samuel 11:1). And it was then he got into all the trouble with Bathsheba.

God challenged Isobel that day, and she and her husband proceeded to go to Tibet.

I read that and prayed, "Lord, don't let me get comfortable—ever. Help me not to 'settle down'—at least *inside*—until I settle down in Heaven. Whenever You say to 'Go off to war,' I want to be willing and ready."

God helped me to set new goals that birthday, and it turned out to be an extremely positive milestone for me.

Some people face the trauma of aging as early as thirty. But for most, in the final analysis, old age is undoubtedly the real crisis point and certainly the final winter of our lives.

In some cases, old age itself is a form of God's stripping in our lives, for old age can mean

. . . loneliness—loss of mate, friends, children.
. . . loss of strength and physical capacity.
. . . ill health.
. . . financial difficulties.
. . . job loss and a sense of uselessness.

Could old age be God's final attempt to rub the ugly edges from our lives?

Some people truly get better with age—the J. Oswald Sanders and the Corrie ten Booms of this world. We hear of mathematicians, artists, and writers who "come alive at sixty-five," but we don't see many such examples. On TV, anyone over seventy is likely to be portrayed as a bit eccentric, if not downright senile. Most older people certainly are not depicted as useful citizens. We hear of many retired people who are unhappy and unproductive, who have time on their hands but neither the strength to do volunteer work nor the money to fulfill their dreams of retirement.

Then along comes the extraordinary person such as President Reagan or Dr. Herbert Lockyer, who wrote fifty-two books after he "retired" at sixty-five and before he died at age ninety-five. We take courage from them. Still, Herbert Lockyer was alone those thirty years, having lost his dear wife after she had been a mental invalid for many years. Dr. J. Oswald Sanders has lost two wives and been a widower for many years. So, in spite of the wonderful way in which God used these men, their latter years undoubtedly were filled with loneliness and pain.

But what about us ordinary people?

I am coming to believe that old age is God's concluding attempt to make us like Jesus. As in other stages of life, some allow Him to do it, others resist Him all the way.

❖ ❖ ❖

Clara (not her real name, of course) was a small, wrinkled, wealthy, feisty woman. Her wealth and position no doubt gave her a secure anvil on which to sharpen her tongue. And sharpen it she did. Then, in quick succession, a daughter-in-law turned on her, her husband died, and finally her health failed. Clara ended her days in a nursing home. But to my knowledge her sharp tongue and feisty nature grew worse as the days passed.

I have to contrast Clara's life with the lives of my mother-in-law and father-in-law. I'm glad my mother-in-law's name is Ruth, because she does remind me of the biblical Ruth whose heart was turned toward God.

Three years of hiccups racked my father-in-law, Clarence, or "Clancy" as some called him. He would have a few days rest, and then more days and nights of convulsive hiccups that shook his whole body. But we never heard him complain.

His wife, pained from watching him suffer, grew braver and stronger in the Lord. Their courageous smiles warmed me as I observed them living on a limited income but rejoicing in what they *did* have rather than complaining about what they did not have.

When God took Dad Home, I watched Mom shine forth as gold. Always a prayer warrior, she now had time to pray two or more hours a day, study God's Word more deeply, and continue reaching out to people.

Both Clara and my mother-in-law endured a stripping process. But only one of them came forth as gold.

Many times I have asked God not to let me become a burden to our only child in my old age so that, if Jack is gone, she won't have to bear that responsibility. I remember telling this to a dear older friend, Morena. And I recall clearly her response. She pointed her short index finger into my face and said sternly, "Carole, how do you know that that may be the *very* way God uses to teach Lynn about Himself?"

I recently shared this with Doris, whose mother has Alzheimer's disease and is quickly losing her capabilities. With shining face, Doris agreed with Morena. "As hard as it's been, I wouldn't trade anything for what I've learned through mother's illness."

I sighed.

I would like to claim verses such as Psalm 92:14-15: "They [the righteous] will still bear fruit in old age, they will stay fresh and green, proclaiming, 'The LORD is upright.'" I would like to answer yes to the questions asked in Job 12:12: "Is not wisdom found among the aged? Does not long life bring understanding?" But as I look around, I see our culture itself mitigating against respecting the wisdom and understanding of older people. In most professions, our youth-oriented society doesn't know how to use the experience of elders. And many people who retire accept this judgment without a struggle. Our generation expects retirement to mean a perpetual vacation because, perhaps subconsciously, we think older people are not useful anymore and are merely trying to enjoy life before they die.

Just recently we were with friends who showed us a beautiful retirement center with four parts to it:

First stage—a lovely condo where you have (almost) independent living but can go to the main dining room for one or all meals.

Second stage—you move to a studio in the main complex, which also houses the hospital, and you eat all meals in the dining room or have them served in your room.

Third stage—you graduate to full-time nursing/hospital care.

Fourth stage—you are placed in your cemetery plot.

What a setup! Secure and comfortable and final. The existence of that retirement center isn't what troubles me. I object to the *attitude* within and without the walls of that place—the unquestionable acceptance that old age is the time of life when one should be made as comfortable as possible until one is troweled into the grave.

That disturbs me!

If we all bought that philosophy, the world would have missed Einstein's theory of relativity, the painting of Grandma Moses, Colonel Sander's Kentucky Fried Chicken, and most of the works of Herbert Lockyer and J. Oswald Sanders. And we would have, in one great brush stroke, swept aside almost every leader in the Old Testament.

Some countries outside the United States are wiser in their attitudes about aging. In the Far East and in Africa, gray hair is honored and respected. I smiled the other day when I received a letter from a girl in China addressing me as "Aunty Carole"—an address of respect for an older woman. So perhaps the difficult process of old age is more pronounced in countries with a youth-oriented mindset. But for whatever reason, God uses the multiplied problems of age to school many in a crash course for Heaven. Yet our outlook is so different from His.

> God says, "Gray hair is a crown of splendor."
>> We say, "Dye it and get a youthful cut."

> God says, "Parents are the pride of their children."
>> We say, "Children are the pride of their parents."

> God says, "Grandchildren are the crown to the aged."

We say, "Grandchildren are the joy of the aged."[2] (I have to admit, in this last coupling, *both* are true!)

Isn't it just like God to take the negative attitudes of our culture, along with other natural processes, and weave them together to achieve His purposes?

Unless God takes us Home earlier than the average length of life, each of us faces getting older. Face lifts can't stop it, exercise can't delay it, health foods can't negate it. Oh, those things may slow down the process on the outside, but one day keeps marching inexorably after another no matter what we do, bringing us, each twenty-four hours, one day closer to our end on earth.

So how do we handle it, this stripping of old age?

Well, first of all, a sense of humor helps.

I just received a copy of a newspaper clipping about a ninety-two-year-old Danish lady now living in Ohio. Johanna Bauer, the caption under her picture proclaims, loves life. "If you write anything about me, be sure you put the word 'spiritual' next to my name," she said firmly. "I spent my time in the United States [the last seventy-two years] in service of the Lord."

The article said, "Her formula for a long and happy life is to be able to accept change and to remain active and interested in people. And always, she said, look at the positive side of everything."

The reporter told the readers that before she said goodbye, Mrs. Bauer gave a copy of this poem to her. I want to share it with you:

Two frogs fell into a deep cream bowl
One was an optimistic soul

But the other took the gloomy view
"We shall drown," he said without more ado
So with a last despairing cry
He flung out his legs and said goodbye.

Quote the other frog with a merry grin
"I can't get out but I won't give in
I will just swim around 'til my strength is spent
And then I will die the more content."

Bravely he swam 'til it would seem
His struggles began to churn the cream
On top of the butter he gladly stopped
And out of the bowl he gaily hopped.

What is the moral?
It's easily found:
If you can't hop out,
Keep swimming around.[3]

We can all keep swimming around!

It is delightful to find an older person still laughing. On the last trip to the hospital before the Lord took Dad Home, he was to have one final surgery by a surgeon he had not met. When the eminent and businesslike surgeon entered his room and introduced himself, Dad said saucily, "How do I know you're a surgeon? Have you got any credentials?" The surgeon laughed heartily, and he and Dad became fast friends. Even when facing surgery, Dad hung on to his marvelous sense of humor.

❖ ❖ ❖

Forsythias like bursts of sunshine blazed against the barnyard fence that spring day in Ithaca, New

York, as the conference broke to enjoy lunch. Several of us took our sack lunches outside to enjoy the day, and after spreading a paper napkin on a rough wooden step, I sat down and began to devour my sandwich.

When I stood up, however, my skirt stuck briefly to the step and, to my dismay upon examination, I saw several black tar spots on my almost-new light aqua skirt.

I groaned. Two hundred women were about to gaze on that skirt as I mounted the platform to speak. No way to hide the ugly black spots.

The church's auditorium was divided into two sections. One group of women had full view of people on the platform, the other only a side view. So, before the "I wonder if she knows she has something on the back of her skirt?" murmurs began, I turned to both sides of the auditorium and displayed, in all of its awesome splotchiness, the back of my dress, explaining, "Just wanted you all to stop wondering. Yes, I know I have tar on the back of my skirt." Then we proceeded with the meeting.

After the conference, one elderly white-haired lady with a twinkle in her eye, brushed past me, leaned close, and whispered low, "Do you know you have something on the back of your skirt?"

I hooted! Thank God for aged sages who have kept on laughing through the years.

Aside from a needed sense of humor, it seems imperative for us to keep a clear view of our life goals—or at least what our life goals *should* be.

In 1983, Dr. Bob Munger—a Presbyterian minister, seminary professor, and author—found out he had intestinal cancer and had to face major surgery. He said in an interview that he was prepared for it in a sense; he felt he was already living on borrowed time, having been a diabetic for thirty-six years. He got through the surgery O.K., but as he was pulling out of it, he came down with hepatitis from the blood transfusion and had to return to the hospital for three weeks. Just as he was reentering active life, he had a heart attack and went back to the same hospital. Every three or four days, he would have another attack, and finally he had bypass surgery. When asked what he learned in that dark period, he answered,

> In Philippians 1, Paul says, "It's my earnest expectation that now as always Christ shall be magnified in my body, whether it be by life or by death. For me to live is Christ and to die is gain." God could glorify himself either by my living or my dying. If my life goal was to honor Christ, then I could do it either way. It resolved the tension for me. It wasn't all that important that I live. It was for my loved ones I felt pain.
>
> That realization has freed me, now in this stage of my life, to enjoy the journey. Why not, if God's in charge? Why take so seriously our aches and pains or our problems and difficulties? Why is that so all important?
>
> Maturity is adjustment to reality. The mature person in Christ is the one who has faced and adjusted to the facts of the real Christ. It's not your happy experience; it's the fact that the real world of God is still firm, and you're in it.[4]

Maturity—physical and spiritual—is what it's all about. In old age, we have long since matured physically. But to mature spiritually in the way God would have us takes all of our lives.

If our life goal is to honor and glorify Christ, then the agonies of age can be taken in stride.

Endurance and perseverance are most difficult when we are physically weak, of course. Yet that is exactly when we need them most. The beautiful thing is that God doesn't leave us on our own to endure or to persevere. Colossians 1:11-12 reads, "Being strengthened with all power according to his glorious might so that you may have great endurance and patience, and joyfully giving thanks to the Father, who has qualified you." One key to be able to do this is found in Hebrews 12:3: "Consider him who *endured* such opposition from sinful men, so that you will not grow weary and lose heart" (italics mine).

Most likely, each of us will face what we euphemistically refer to as "the golden years." Oh that we will face these years with head held high, knowing that we are each day one step closer to graduation; that each lesson is for our best; that, if God chooses to use age to strip us of excess baggage, it will be done with love to prepare us for His eternity.

A sense of humor, a clear life goal, and a right perspective on the winter of our lives will help us through victoriously.

◆ ◆ ◆

"What a jewel of a day, Lord!" I breathed as I looked at the cloudless sky and contemplated our plans for the hours ahead. We would leave this little cabin by the edge of the McKenzie River, travel northeast through the mountains of Oregon, play golf at Black Butte, and then settle in at Sun River for two more days of rest between conferences.

"It's as if . . . well, Lord . . . it's as if You're placing a small, beautiful jewel in the mosaic of my life on this day."

In my mind I pictured that mosaic. I observed as the Lord took a precious stone to place it . . . where? Well, probably somewhere down in the lower right-hand corner—for to me, that is where these after-fifty years of my life fit in.

But no! God is placing His jewel in the middle of the design. And I saw in my mind a picture that still needed to be finished *at the center.*

The Lord whispered to my heart, "I'm finishing your life-mosaic, Carole, with the pieces right at the heart. And the last day of your life on earth, your graduation day into Heaven, will be the very center-most piece."

I smiled as I visualized God placing it there with a pristine "ping" and light bursting from it. I realized then that subconsciously I had imagined that last day of life as a "plunk," as perhaps weak and ill, I slipped into the realms of Heaven.

Then I stepped back to view the mosaic, some parts iridescent, some parts brilliant, some parts dark. But, like an opaque opal, even the dark parts shimmered with a deep inner beauty when His light was reflected.

It occurred to me on that lovely morning that God never places a day in the life of a Christian with a "plunk." He always "pings!" Because Christ is *in* us, because God is *for* us, because the triune God delights in our days, I don't think *He* ever "plunks," even when days look dull, routine, ugly, painful, and we view our lives as a "plunk." He "pings" even when we plunk!

He says, "I do all things well." Ping!

"I'm in *this day,* and I love you." Ping!

"I'm working in your life." Ping!

"This too will make you like Jesus." Ping!

Since that day sitting by the McKenzie River, I have stopped contemplating these autumn (perhaps even winter days—only God knows) of my life as "bottom corner" days. They are *center* days, and someday the last one is going to chime into place with a final, wonderful, celestial, graduation *Ping!*

I'm ready.

NOTES:

1. Annie Komorny, "Rage," *Good Housekeeping*, April 1988, page NC2.
2. See Proverbs 16:31, 17:6.
3. Author and source unknown.
4. Donald Bubno, interviewer, "Fifty Years of Ministry and Going Strong," *Leadership Magazine*, Summer 1986, page 86.

CHAPTER 9

DESOLATION:
Losing the Sense of God's Presence

◆

Lord, why are you standing aloof and far away?
Why do you hide when I need you the most?
(PSALM 10:1, TLB)

I sat on a rock in the dry creek bed. Dry-eyed. Numb. Bewildered.

The heat shimmered off the rocks in waves, but I was oblivious to the hot sun on my face. In fact, I felt nothing. And that was my problem. For I desperately wanted to feel—to have my heart weep, or rejoice, or at least be *aware*. Instead, as I looked inside me in a detached sort of way, I saw nothing and felt nothing at all.

I had been this way for weeks. I could not *feel* God's presence in any part of my mind, soul, or spirit. There was a blank—an internal nothingness that left me unable to perceive emotions of any kind. I felt dead inside. Even on the outside, I was only going through the motions of living.

A number of factors had led to this point in my life: a move; my father's sudden death at fifty-seven (he had lived less than two weeks after leukemia was diagnosed); being plunged into an intense ministry situation where my output exceeded my intake. But none of those facts, separately or together, was enough to cause the void in my spirit. As the days and weeks marched into months, I grew more and more desperate. I read my Bible with increasing anxiety. I prayed and pleaded with God to no avail.

I also felt like the world's greatest hypocrite! Sitting on a rock in that dry creek bed, I remonstrated with God, "Lord, I can't go on like this! Here I am married to a full-time Christian worker. I'm leading two Bible studies, meeting with several individuals for discipling, memorizing Scripture, praying—Lord, I'm doing all the right *things*—and harder than ever. So why don't I *feel* Your presence?

"I'm telling people of Your joy, but I don't have it myself. I'm telling people of Your peace, but where is it? I'm telling people You will never leave them, but I feel as if *You have left me!*

"Lord, I'll go out of my mind if You don't do *something*. I can't keep on going through the motions any longer." My voice dwindled and was silent.

Then I waited and listened.

But God was silent.

Wearily, I trudged back home.

During that time I discovered, and I am still unearthing the fact, that I was not alone in my experience.

David Needham in his book *Close to His Majesty* has a chapter entitled "Trembling at His Faithfulness," but instead of writing of the dramatic stories of God's miracles in Scripture, Needham says,

We are going to walk through a long dark tunnel with a man who went to his death with dreams unfulfilled. A man with enough evidence to convince any jury that his God had failed him. Yet a man who was the inspiration for one of the most famous hymns of Christendom, "Great Is Thy Faithfulness."[1]

He then quotes some of the wonderful promises of God to Jeremiah such as Jeremiah 1:18-19 (NASB): "Now behold, I have made you today as a fortified city, and as a pillar of iron and as walls of bronze against the whole land. . . . And they will fight against you, but they will not overcome you, for I am with you to deliver you."

Jeremiah was given a seemingly impossible job, but as Needham writes:

A tough job? Yes, but with such full divine protection plus guaranteed deliverance, he couldn't lose . . . or could he?

In the years that followed, Jeremiah would experience imprisonment, beatings, loneliness (he was forbidden to marry), rejection, attempted assassinations, public ridicule, and— most painful of all—the apparent failure of God's faithfulness.[2]

Jeremiah cries, "Why has my pain been perpetual and my wound incurable, refusing to be healed? Wilt Thou indeed be to me like a deceptive stream with water that is unreliable?" (Jeremiah 15:18, NASB).

The weeping prophet had cause! Where was the fulfillment of the many promises God had given him?

Fortunately, God does not deal with most of us

the way He dealt with Jeremiah. However, both the stripping processes that occur when a person feels divested of God's presence and the wondering concerning His ways can be devastating for us.

Not only have I endured times of desolation because God seemed absent, I have also spent months questioning His ways. A few years ago, I realized a strange phenomenon was taking place in my mid-life years: God's dramatic answers to prayer seemed fewer, further between, and I couldn't help but wonder why. Wouldn't it seem that as a person knows God longer and more intimately, more spectacular manifestations of God would occur? But no. For me, just the opposite was true. Why? I remember reading biographies of several men of God who had testified to this same phenomenon, and I wondered about it then. Did other factors enter in? Was it a matter of one's not asking, or trusting, or expecting God to act? I had to conclude that those factors were valid to a degree. But I knew too that this was not always the case.

Jeremiah came to the end of his life with no answers at all.

That, of course, is the whole point of this kind of stripping—of this kind of trusting. God is teaching us a unique lesson, and it sifts down to this: God is God whether we feel Him or not. God's promises are true whether we experience them or not. His ways are far above our comprehension. He is too big for us to understand, to assess. Whether or not we hear or feel Him, He says we are to *trust* Him.

I probably should end this chapter right here. For the essence of this lesson comes in the seeming endlessness of the dilemma.

However, for those of us who are not Jeremiahs

(and I say, "Thank You, Lord!"), God leads us *through* these times and does give us some insight into the reasons for this kind of desolation.

So let's take the two difficulties—questioning His ways in our lives and losing the sense of God's presence—and look for some possible help.

Does God sometimes change His methods of manifesting Himself to us as we pass through various stages of life? Yes, I think so, and I think there is a tremendous reason for His doing this.

It seems as though He is underlining a message to me as I get closer to the end of life's journey. He appears to be saying, "Carole, as a young Christian, you needed Me to reveal Myself to you through what I *did* for you. But now, I want you to know *Me*, My character, My love. I want your eyes to be on who I am rather than on what I can or will do for you. In years past I've shown you My dramatic love. Now is the time for you to know My deep love."

It clicked then. It's a bit like marriage. Jack and I have been married for thirty-eight plus years at the time I write this. If you were to ask me if our love is the same now as that magical moment when we walked down the aisle and exchanged our vows, I would without hesitation say, "Why no, of course not. I thought I loved Jack then as much as one human being could love another. But, truthfully, I didn't even know what love was all about."

Yet there were dramatic (and romantic) demonstrations of our love that first year in greater number than in this, the thirty-ninth year of our lives together.

Now please don't misunderstand me. Jack and I still work at the dramatic and the romantic. Those aspects of love are fun, and we don't ever want to lose them. It's just that we don't *need* such displays as often in order to be assured of the other's love. Day by day we experience deep love much more than dramatic love.

I experienced Jack's deep love for me just this week.

Jack and I rented a condo at a lovely resort for a much-needed rest. But the unit had a lock-off bedroom that, the day after we moved in, was rented to two men whom we kept running into in the tiny confined common hallway. They were strange men from whose room came weird and terrible sounds. I don't think of myself as a fearful person, but to me the atmosphere was full of, well, *evil*, and I grew increasingly depressed.

Many husbands would have (1) laughed, (2) been scornful, or (3) been disgusted. Instead, Jack spent the day looking for another condo with me and moving all our things from this third floor walk-up to another second floor walk-up. And he did it with love and tenderness, showing absolutely no disgust or frustration over the lost vacation day. Not dramatic, romantic love, but deep, quiet love.

To me that unselfish act said more than several bouquets of long-stemmed roses or expensive candlelight dinners. It reveals Jack's character in a way that a moonlight cruise never could.

Of course, I love to hear about some romantic adventure when a husband or wife whisks his or her spouse off to an exotic hide-a-way weekend. One can live on that for months! But such an act is valid *only* if the character of that husband or wife continues to reinforce the dramatic act of love by daily kindness, consideration, and truthfulness.

You see, love *can* survive without the dramatic. But it will drown without the deep, steady love that is shown by godly characteristics. That's the way it is in marriage.

In a sense, I think God is showing me a similar truth about Himself in these later years of my life. Even so, the dramatic miracles still happen and wow! They are exciting to experience and to tell.

Just a couple of months ago a dear friend related to me that two days before she was to fly out to a long-anticipated conference in Colorado, she inadvertently put her personal prayer and Bible study schedular notebook on the top of her car, and it fell off somewhere during a thirty-mile drive to her daughter's school party. Along with everything else, she had put her specially-priced no-chance-of-repurchasing airline tickets in the notebook. When she realized the notebook was missing, she combed the neighborhood, praying it had fallen off the car close to her home. She asked children to scour neighboring yards, but they only came up with a few smeared pages, which were torn, run over by cars, and wet because of rain in the night. She prayed. Nothing. Just as she was about to give up searching—and consequently going to the conference—the Lord spoke to her heart from the Scripture about the woman who swept her house clean looking for the lost coin (Luke 15:8-10). So she kept hunting.

It was almost dark (the day before she was to leave) when she noted a trash can sitting in front of a home whose residents were away on vacation. The trash had been picked up that noon, but she felt constrained to look into that can. There was nothing in it except one white, folded sheet of paper stuck to the bottom of the can. She left it, then was prompted to return, turn the can on its side, and crawl in to get that folded paper. It was her letter of invitation to the conference and, folded neatly inside, her airline tickets! (They hadn't even been *together* in her notebook!) What joy and praise filled her heart. She had experienced God's very special working for one of His children. Yes, miracles still *do* happen. God still can—and does—accomplish miracles. For me too! But not as often. Not as dramatic.

As years go by, I think God is revealing His love to me more by the everyday *being* kind of love than the spectacular *doing* kind of love. It is His character He wants me to know and love more than my desiring what He can and will do for me.

One vital aspect of this is the tremendous lesson in trusting God when we don't feel Him or see Him or hear Him.

Remember the story of Peter when he was washing his nets after fishing all night without success? (See Luke 5:1-5.) Christ told Peter to go into deep water and let down the nets for a catch. Peter replied, "Master, we've worked hard all night and haven't caught anything. *But because you say so*, I will let down the nets" (verse 5, italics mine).

As you know, Peter and his crew caught such a large number of fish that their nets began to break and they had to signal for help! How many times in our lives does it boil down to that? *Because You say so.* Period. End of discussion.

One very important ingredient in this—in the acceptance of all of life really—is letting the truth of Psalm 16:5 grip our souls. David exclaimed, "LORD, you have assigned me my portion and my cup; you have made my lot secure." I've been giving a lot of thought to this verse lately.

God has assigned me my portion. I describe *portion* as those factors in my life over which I have no choice. The portion God assigned me includes being born Caucasian, in the United States, of Christian parents, the middle child of three. He assigned me my height, my body structure, the color of my hair, eyes, skin, my propensity for good health, my personality, my talents and gifts. I had no choice about any of the above or about a vast list of other givens. They are my portion.

I have obvious *choices* within that portion. I can choose to ruin my health, change my hair color, or not develop my gifts. But I need to remember that it is God who has assigned me my portion.

He has also assigned me my *cup*. To me, the cup is life's experiences—good, bad, and indifferent—to which I'm exposed. Christ prayed that the cup of the Cross would be taken from Him, the experience of all that the Cross entailed.

My cup has included the experiences of having an increasingly senile grandmother live with us in my growing-up years; of having my younger sister die a slow, painful death of leukemia; of having times of great financial difficulty; of floods in our basement.

But *God* has assigned me my cup. However, in a very real sense, *I have to drink from it.* I have no control over the cup God hands me, but I have choices as to how much, or how deeply, I will drink from it. Our tendency, like a child turning his face away from bitter-tasting medicine, is to drink as little as possible.

God assigned a bitter cup to Jeremiah, described in Lamentations 3. Look at some of the troubles Jeremiah lamented—not troubles that "just happened" but ones that *God caused*. Jeremiah said God

> . . . drove him away and made him walk in
> darkness rather than light (verse 2).

. . . turned His hand against him again and
    again, all day long (verse 3).
. . . broke his bones, made his skin and flesh
    grow old (verse 4).
. . . surrounded him with bitterness and hard-
    ship (verse 5).
. . . made him dwell in darkness like those long
    dead (verse 6).
. . . imprisoned him—weighed him down with
    chains (verse 7).
. . . shut out his prayer (verse 8).
. . . mangled him and left him without help
    (verse 11).
. . . made him the target for His arrows (verse
    12).
. . . made him the object of ridicule (verse 14).
. . . broke his teeth (verse 16).
. . . took away his peace (verse 17).
. . . took away his prosperity (verse 17).
. . . took away his splendor (verse 18).
. . . took away *hope* (verse 18).

That's quite a list!

Jeremiah concluded his list by saying, "I remember my affliction and my wandering, the bitterness
and the gall. I well remember them, and my soul is
downcast within me" (verses 19-20).

Well, I guess! Wouldn't your soul be?

But this prophet didn't stop there. In a crescendo of praise, he lifted his heart:

Yet this I call to mind and therefore I have hope:
Because of the LORD's great love we are not
consumed, for his compassions never fail. They
are new every morning; great is your faithful-

ness. I say to myself, "The LORD is my portion; therefore I will wait for him." (verses 21-24, italics mine)

The Lord had assigned Jeremiah his portion just as He assigns portions to each of us. But Jeremiah had learned a tremendous secret, which you and I need to learn and cling to with every fiber of our souls. It is this: Not only has the Lord *assigned* me my portion, but the Lord Himself *is* my portion. The psalmist said it well: "You are my *portion*, O LORD; I have promised to obey your words" (Psalm 119:57). And in the passage above, Jeremiah asserted, "The LORD is my portion; therefore I will wait for him" (Lamentations 3:24).

When the portion the Lord assigns us in life seems to include brokenness, "prisons" (oh, I hate those prisons of situations I don't like, of circumstances I abhor), aging, yes even the loss of hope, the glorious shining truth still remains, *the Lord is my portion.* "I cry to you, O LORD; I say, 'You are my refuge, my portion in the land of the living'" (Psalm 142:5).

The secret of survival—both when we question God's methods as well as when God's presence is not felt or perceived—is the same for us as it was for Jeremiah. He called to mind certain truths that gave him hope. What was it he deliberately remembered?

Take a moment right now, turn to Lamentations 3, read verses 22-38, and be blessed along with me. Note the facts Jeremiah deliberately called to mind.

This list far outweighs the previous one!

Jeremiah remembered that God's love and His faithfulness are *great*, that His compassions not only never fail (they are constant and eternal whether we see them or not) but also are *new* every morning, fresh and real. He considered that the Lord is good to those whose hope is in Him and who seek Him. Then he recognized that the Lord sees and is in control of *everything*—of the calamities and the blessings—that we can't change a thing (so we might as well relax!) but that as we *wait*, God will make sense of it all.

Jeremiah was assigned a bitter cup, and he drank it fully. I am convinced, however, that many of us refuse to drink from the cup God has for us—or we only sip.

He can assign me affliction; but I can reject the lessons. He can assign me love; but I can refuse it. He can assign me (and does) the river of His delights (see Psalm 36:8), His Word; but I can keep my lips *tightly* closed! He can assign me my place and my portion; and I can either squirm, claw, and struggle or I can *rest*. The choice is mine.

The prophet Jeremiah has told us the secret of drinking fully of God's cup. First, we are to KNOW (see Lamentations 3:22-23)—know that God is in control, that He is great, that He loves us.

Second we are to SEEK (see verse 25)—seek God with our whole heart and soul and strength.

And third we are to WAIT (see verse 26)—wait for however long it takes for God to act. That's hard! I hate to wait! But God says if we wait we will be blessed (see Isaiah 30:18); we will have the door opened to us; we will see His work in our lives. We *will* again experience the joy and delight of His presence.

An act of the will—obeying God in these three areas—brings *hope* out of hopelessness (see Lamentations 3:21).

❖ ❖ ❖

Now, let me tell you the end of the story with which I began this chapter.

I was desperate. Every day I cried and pleaded with God to tell me what was wrong in my life. I searched my heart for sin, praying Psalm 139:23-24. I spent extra time reading the Bible, and I prayed longer and harder than usual. But God was silent.

Until one night.

God gave me the enlightenment I needed through a little book called *We Would See Jesus* by Roy and Revel Hession. I'm sure if I had read that book at any other time in my life, it would have been just another good book. But God had me read it at a time when some of its truth jumped off of the pages right into my life.

The authors talk about the fact that today we don't hear much about the need to *see* God.

Two emphases stand out today.

First of all, instead of stressing holiness in order to *see* God, the emphasis is on service *for* God. We have come to think of the Christian life as consisting in serving God as fully and as efficiently as we can. Techniques and methods, by which we hope to make God's message known, have become the important thing. To carry out this service we need power, and so instead of a longing for God, our longing is for power to serve Him more effectively.

Then there tends to be today an emphasis on the seeking of inner spiritual experiences. While so many Christians are content to live at a very low level, it is good that some do become concerned about their Christian lives, and it is right that they should. However, the concern arises not so much from a hunger for God, but from a longing to find an inner experience of

happiness, joy, and power, and we find ourselves looking for "it", rather than God
Himself.[3]

Later they write, "To concentrate on service and
activity for God may often actively thwart our attain-
ing of the true goal, God Himself."[4]

One night—very late—after reading that book,
two truths broke open my heart, and God's love and
presence flooded back in. The first truth, put very
simply, was that, up to this time in my Christian life, I
had been coming to God *for something*—for His
peace, His love, His power, His grace—and He had
let me do that. But now He was wanting a more
mature relationship. He was wanting me to come to
Him *just for Himself* and not for anything He would
give me. Sounds so simple, doesn't it? But in my life,
what was happening was so subtle I hadn't even
realized it. Every morning I would pray for blessing,
for wisdom, for peace, for joy, for love. *For something.*

I thought of Lynn, then five years old. I didn't
mind her running to me for her needs or her wants. I
understood her child's mind when she would give me
a big hug and then ask for something. It was O.K. She
was only five. But I realized that if, at twenty-one, the
only time Lynn came to me or told me she loved me or
wanted to spend time with me was when she wanted
something from me, well, I wouldn't be very happy
with that.

God was telling me that very thing. He wanted
me to come to Him because I loved Him and wanted
to be with Him, not just for something He would give
me. Of course, He had promised peace, joy, and
blessings, and He would give them. But my motives
needed to be purified.

The second truth was that, unconsciously, I had begun to think that the more I prayed and studied and memorized Scripture, the closer I would be to God. I had it all backwards. That night I saw clearly that none of those spiritual disciplines was the way to God. Jesus Christ is the way to God. And because I have Jesus, I couldn't be any closer to God! He lives in me. He loves me as He loves His Son. He has chosen me, and He delights in me. I can't *earn* closeness by any of the "mechanics" of the Christian life.

Of course as my eyes were opened to the fact that Jesus is *the* way and the *only* way, I recognized that Christ will lead me to the disciplines of prayer and Bible study that I may see Him more clearly and know Him more intimately, but they are not the way I get "close" to the Father.

The scales dropped from my spiritual eyes, and I fell weeping before my God. The joy of His presence flooded my spirit once again, and I praised His name.

David Needham says worship is seeing a God "too big" and saying "Wow!" or "Gasp."[5] I agree.

That night—and may it be soon for you, my friend, if you are void of the presence of God—I saw a God too big. And I said, "Wow!"

NOTES:
1. David Needham, *Close to His Majesty* (Portland: Multnomah, 1987), pages 91-92.
2. Needham, *Close to His Majesty*, page 92.
3. Roy and Revel Hession, *We Would See Jesus* (Fort Washington, Pa.: Christian Literature Crusade, 1958), pages 10-11.
4. Hession, *We Would See Jesus*, page 14.
5. Needham, *Close to His Majesty*, page 149.

CHAPTER 10

TRIALS UPON TRIALS:
Losing Understanding

◆

All day long they surround me like a flood;
they have completely engulfed me.
(PSALM 88:17)

t 7:20 a.m. on Thursday, September 19, 1985, an earthquake shattered Mexico City, hitting the downtown tourist and government centers. Viewers were shocked as pictures on TV showed the Regis Hotel demolished in seconds to a pile of rubble. Thousands died instantly; others were trapped, injured, and left homeless.

At 7:19 a.m. in a room on the ninth floor of the Hotel del Prado across the street from the Regis Hotel, a blond-haired young man prepared to step into a shower. His wife and two children remained in bed, tired from packing and traveling the four hours from their home in Guanajuato the day before. They all were looking forward to returning to the United States for a time of needed rest and recuperation.

Suddenly, the room began to move. Tim thought, *I'm having a dizzy spell* and sat down quickly on the edge of the tub. Suddenly his wife, Lynn, burst through the door shouting, "It's an earthquake!" They snatched the children from bed, but were unable to get to the doorway before being thrown to the floor by the violent motion. When the shaking finally sub- sided, they dressed themselves and their son hastily, leaving with their four-year-old daughter in her pajamas.

Leaving everything else—airline tickets, travel documents, clothes, suitcases—they headed for the emergency stairs. Breathing became difficult as they inched downward, the air thick with plaster dust, causing them to cough and choke. Trying in vain to see through the dust-filled air, they slipped and slid over the debris and lost track of which floor they were on. A security guard appeared through the thick haze on the fourth floor and finally led them from the building.

They stumbled to a nearby park where hundreds were gathering, some with only a towel wrapped around them, others still in nightclothes. Finally gathering their courage, they walked the mile or so to the American Embassy where they were sheltered briefly and then found their way to the apartment of friends just outside the devastated area.

For two days they survived the aftershocks, a second quake, the horrors of the devastation. Then miraculously, on temporary exit visas, they boarded a plane for Denver, rented a car and arrived at our doorstep, ragged, exhausted, with a small shopping bag as their only luggage. Our daughter, her husband, our grandchildren Eric and Sunny were safe. They were home. We shed tears of joy and relief together.

It wasn't until some hours later that I stopped to ask *why*. As the ministry had grown in Guanajuato, Tim tried to do more and more and finally had come to the verge of physical and emotional exhaustion. I had prayed that God would smooth the way before them, alleviate the hassle of more frayed nerves. Instead, they ended up in the middle of a terrible earthquake. "I really don't think they needed *that*, Lord!" I chided.

Isn't that awful? Instead of praising God for their safety, I was complaining!

But God wasn't through yet.

In the weeks to come, Tim had to have a hernia operation, and Lynn discovered she would need a hysterectomy within two years, which meant no more children.

Multiplied trials. Diminished emotional and physical capacity to cope. Were they being stripped by God?

In a sense, yes.

And, oh, did we learn!

◆ ◆ ◆

My friend's first letters from the Philippines lamented, cried, raged. She hated it! She despised the poverty, loathed the heat, detested the cockroaches, abhorred the rats. She wanted out.

She seethed against the military that had ordered her family to this foreign island. This tall, attractive, blonde Swede was forced to live in a land of short, brown-skinned people. She, who loved the cold and snow and seasons, had to dwell in heat, humidity, and mold. She, who loved to dig among tulips and daffodils, laugh with friends, and minister to neighbors, was transplanted to a land of carabaos (water buffalo), thatched-roof houses, and roads jammed with jeepneys and crowded buses. She hated the land, the situation, the circumstances of her life. She, who longed more than anyone I had ever known for roots, was uprooted and transplanted. Swiftly, violently, irrevocably.

For weeks . . . months . . . her letters beat a desperate message of despair, exhaustion, and discouragement. Methodically, God had stripped away her security and supports.

◆ ◆ ◆

Another letter came from a friend whose life at that moment sounded like the Perils of Pauline. She eloquently described what was going on:

> The preceding year has been, in many ways, the worst single year I've ever experienced and yet one of the most glorious years in terms of personal growth and of beginning to comprehend the depth of God's intense love affair with me. . . . It's been a year I would never have wished on myself—but one I would not trade for anything!
>
> . . . Last year I wrote of my discovery that God was more concerned with molding my character and making me Christ-like than He was with giving me a comfortable, worry-free life. Little did I know that He and I were about to enroll in a crash-course of intense character building!

Sherry tells of rushing to the bed of her mother who suffered two heart attacks and was not expected to live the night, but rallied. Sherry was able to return home. Two nights after her mother was released from the hospital, she suddenly collapsed and died.

Then when Sherry's dad was able to visit her family more often and she was getting to know him better, he suffered a mild stroke while at their home, which left him hospitalized with an inability to balance himself and a slight speech impairment. Sherry reacted: "It seemed such a cruel joke life was playing to take his health just when he was finally free to begin to enjoy the few remaining years he had left!"

But more was to come:

> Shortly before Dad was to be released from the hospital to our care at home, Tom [her husband] and I decided to go on a little getaway biking weekend with the kids. On a quiet flat stretch of country road in Michigan, the front fork of our tandem suddenly snapped in half, cartwheeling both of us over the handlebars. Tom (gallant husband that he is) laid his body on the pavement for me and literally "broke" my fall as I landed first on him before skidding down the blacktop. I only sustained minor scrapes. Tom wasn't so fortunate. His broken hand healed relatively fast, but the collarbone broke into three pieces, which even after months in a brace refused to reconnect and heal properly.

Tom couldn't lie down for eight weeks. Months of therapy began and depression resulted from slow progress. Adding to all that, their oldest son, after one week into his senior year of high school, suffered a grand mal seizure. It was back to the hospital routine for a week of thorough testing, which confirmed he did indeed have epilepsy and would need to be on medication the rest of his life. Her son's driving license suspended, Sherry became the family taxi, which included getting up at midnight to fetch her son from work. But then her son forgot to take his medicine and had a second seizure. Furious with himself, the disease, the medicine, he went into a state of denial, and all kinds of problems erupted.

And they both learned! Sherry tells it graphically:

When I turned into a raving nag, David, of course, did what 18-year-olds do—he chose the issue of his sleep and pills over which to declare his war of independence and it was clear he was determined to fight it to the death, even if it meant *his own*. Again when I quit shouting long enough at God to listen, I heard God's whisper, "Try surrender. Shut up. Listen to Me and button your lip." (If you don't think God talks that way, try reading Isaiah 41:4, Eph. 2:14-16, 22-26.) It is one of the hardest battles I've ever fought with myself to stand silently by and see my beautiful, talented, intelligent, cooperative, mature child that I've loved and nurtured for 18 years to the brink of adulthood, self-destructing—and be powerless to stop it. As I tried it God's way and backed off, allowing David to learn hard lessons for himself and not sheltering him from the consequences of his poor choices, I discovered some important truths: (1) David's choices weren't always poor. They were *different* from mine, but not necessarily *wrong*! And much of his logic was well-thought-out, if not always based on accurate data. (2) Some lessons MUST be learned for oneself. Better he learn them now than next fall when he is away at college with no support group. (3) Growing up involves being allowed to make wrong choices, learn from them, and take responsibility for the consequences. It's OK to make mistakes. (4) I began to watch David's actions and see a clear reflection of *my own* attitudes. David would accuse me of trying to enslave him in rigid rules and not letting him do things (like downhill skiing the day after a seizure) *just because I didn't want him to have any fun*! And when I felt the hurt of his questioning my motives, I suddenly knew what it is like for God, my heavenly parent, my Father, when I rebel against His rules. He created me and knows what is best for me and gives me rules of conduct that protect me from self-destructive behavior—and I accuse Him of cramping my style and taking the "fun" out of life. I want my independence even if I destroy myself in the process! And God gives me free will to go my way.

. . . As I reflect back over 1985, I can't help but hope God is planning a nice long "summer break" for me from this course in Character Building 101 that He seems to have me majoring in . . . but even if it continues, I've seen enough of His faithfulness and provision—and the tremendous good that has come out of the "bad"—to know I can trust Him to lead me through anything that He allows to come my way. . . . I would pick for myself a nice, easy, uneventful *existence*, but in God's limitless creativity, He selects for me exciting *adventures* that stretch my faith to the very limits of my being at times. Whoever thinks that being a Christian is a dull, ho-hum life, "AIN'T NEVER TAKEN GOD'S HAND AND WALKED THROUGH LIFE WITH A DIVINE COMPANION." I pity their loss.

When I received Sherry's letter, I wanted to stand and shout, "The Lord is great and greatly to be praised. For our Lord God is willing to weep with us, hurt for us, cry when we cry, in order to fashion us to be like Him. The Lord God uses His love and power, not to make us comfortable, but to make us conformed. Hallelujah!"

Can you trace the hand of God through His stripping in Sherry's life? One by one God removed the support of her parents, her husband, her eldest son. (I left out the part about the finances, but you can imagine the hospital bills, let alone the expense of her son's beginning college.) But perhaps hardest of all was the stripping of her need to be needed by her son—his rebellion toward her for a time—and the tearing, rending pain caused by having to stand by while she felt he was destroying himself.

Stripped. Taken down to the root of her bruised soul. Why? That God might rebuild and fashion her to be more like the Master.

Four people: Tim, Lynn, Sherry, and my dear friend in the Philippines. Diverse circumstances and yet a common denominator. Each was being divested of buttresses that in their thinking, had held up the bridge of their lives. One by one the supports fell until the only support left was God. But He is enough.

There is a great cliff near our home in Colorado. Suppose one day I decide that cliff is in danger of falling and I need to shore it up. So I spend much time and money building great slanting braces from ground to cliff. After years of shoring up the cliff, one night an earthquake shakes the area, and one by one those props collapse. But the cliff of solid rock stands as it has been standing for millions of years, not one rock dislodged.

We think we are bolstering our lives with supports of health, money, organizations, friends, family, job security, position, reputation. Then one by one those props fall away, or perhaps I should say God pulls them away. We hold our breath, wondering if the whole cliff is going to tumble. But it is solid rock. The supports are comfortable to us. We like the supports, but they are *not necessary* for our survival. And God is not as interested in our comfort as He is in our conformation.

Well, you say, that sounds good, but just knowing I don't need those supports doesn't do it. True. Perhaps a few practical steps will help us when our world seems to be falling apart.

Consider . . . *God never makes mistakes.*

The God who stopped the mouths of lions, the God who brought three Hebrews safely through the fiery furnace without one hair singed, the God who opened the mouth of a donkey to warn a prophet— THAT GOD could have prevented the earthquake in Mexico City. THAT GOD could have caused Uncle Sam to send my friend to a country other than the Philippines. THAT GOD could have prevented Sherry's dad from having a stroke, the tandem from falling apart, injury to her husband, epilepsy to her son. As hard as life is, as ugly as it sometimes seems, *nevertheless* when pain and hurt reach me, they are not accidental or incidental, and therefore *God means them for my good.*

Consider: *God is training us to make life better and to make us better.* Hebrews 12:9 (TLB) clearly states, "Should we not all the more cheerfully submit to God's training so that we can begin really to live?" God is training us so that we can really begin to live! Both now and for all eternity. And He is in the business of making *us* better as well because verse 10 continues, "Our earthly fathers trained us for a few brief years, doing the best for us that they knew how, but God's correction is always right and for our best good, that we may share his holiness." Can you imagine sharing God's holiness? That's incredible! In Christ I have been made holy. In my present life God is working at making me what He has already declared me to be: Holy. Righteous. Godly. Can you imagine the work and training that takes? But He never gets weary in the process. You and I may, but God never does. The process must be kept in the forefront of my mind; or I will lose heart when I've knocked myself out on a project only to have it fail or when I can see absolutely no good reason for what is happening in my life. God is more interested in teaching me through a situation than in using me in a situation. He is interested in both, of course, but He is much more interested in individuals than in the outcome of situations.

We know that in our heads. We just have to let it soak into the fabric of our souls. So many hindrances block our concentration.

Consider *Jesus.* Often we are looking everywhere but to Jesus. Hebrews 12:2-3 tells us: "Let us fix our eyes on Jesus. Consider him who endured such opposition from sinful men, so that you will not grow weary and lose heart."

When we keep our eyes on Jesus, considering what He endured for us, we *won't* lose heart, we won't grow weary of it all. But a great deal of the time, we look anywhere *but* to the Savior.

Remember the story of the rebellious Jewish people wandering the desert? They give us a negative picture of what happens when we don't look to God. God's patience was sorely tried as the Israelites murmured and complained and disobeyed. At one point God became so angry He sent poisonous snakes among them, and many were bitten and died. When they repented, God told Moses to erect a bronze serpent on a tall pole so that when someone was bitten, all they had to do to be saved was to look at the serpent.

Can you imagine that scene? I can just hear some arrogant young man, after being bitten, say, "What a dumb thing! Who would ever believe that looking at a bronze serpent could have any effect? As young and strong as I am, I'll be able to survive this." Two seconds later he is dead.

When we fail to look at Jesus, we look in wrong directions—at self usually. When we look inward, at ourselves, our situations, our inadequacies, we become mired in self-pity. My mother used to say that feeling sorry for oneself was the world's worst indoor sport, and she was right.

Then there are those of us whose eyes are blinded. Our view of Christ is obstructed by our own anger, by bitterness, by discouragement, by frustration, by self-pity. Hebrews 12:1 (TLB) describes some sins as "those sins that wrap themselves . . . tightly around our feet and trip us up." Like a rope tying our ankles together as we start to race, so is that sin we fail to acknowledge and confess. It will trip us up in the race set before us. God may have pointed it out a number of times. He may have spoken to our hearts quite directly saying, "Let Me cut that rope. Let Me free you." But we close our eyes and decide we want to keep that hidden sin, and as a result our view of God is blocked.

Or we may have our eyes *closed*. We are not looking into His Word. We are not praying. We are being "careless about God" (Hebrews 12:16, TLB).

We must contemplate Jesus, whose mercies are "new every morning" (see Lamentations 3:22-23), and long with Hosea, "Oh, that we might know the Lord! Let us press on to know him, and he will respond to us as surely as the coming of dawn or the rain of early spring" (Hosea 6:3, TLB).

Stripping is essential, and suffering is part of that stripping.

Often I have mulled over a conditional promise in Romans 8. Verse 17 reads, "We are heirs . . . of God and co-heirs with Christ, *if* indeed we share in his sufferings in order that we may also share in his glory" (italics mine). As I have thought about that verse, my question was, "Is it possible *not* to share in His sufferings?" I realized the answer was yes. Here's why:

First, we can take a stoic approach to suffering and simply get through it without entering into it—without letting it become a part of us—without learning anything from it.

Second, we can become bitter about it and reject His working in us.

Third, we can run away from it, avoid it if possible, escape it. This escape takes many forms—pills, alcohol, TV. Even depression can be a form of running away if it makes us incapable of coping with or accepting suffering.

The small son of a dear friend fell off a patio deck and landed on his head on a cement slab some twelve feet below. When she reached him, his eyes were rolled back in his head, his skin was gray, and he wasn't breathing. Scooping him up into her arms, she carried him into the dining room, laid him on the floor, and began mouth to mouth resuscitation. It worked! Two hours of tests at the emergency ward failed to find any broken bones. She spent the next three days crying from relief and shaking with thoughts of the "what ifs" and "if I onlys." Calling her mother in another city, she had only started the first sentence when her mother cut her off with, "Oh, don't tell me. I can't bear to think about it."

My friend was crushed. She needed to have her mother's empathy. But even more, her mother needed to share in that suffering. In refusing to listen, she had not only failed to share in her daughter's life (and her daughter felt that rejection), she had also failed to drink the cup of personal suffering; for one of the ways we suffer most is to look on helplessly as we see those we love in pain. And because as we share in the hurts of the Body of Christ (that is, believers in Him), we share in Christ's suffering, this mother was refusing to "suffer with Christ." She was running away from that sharing.

God has given us provisions to make our sharing in Christ's sufferings possible. We are led by the Holy Spirit and have His power to do anything Christ wants us to do. We have the wonderful promise that our present sufferings are not worth comparing to what's coming in future glory. And we have the Spirit Himself praying for us. At this moment I'm *especially* grateful for that last promise, because I think sometimes the way *we* pray and the way the *Spirit* prays are quite different. We pray, "Lord, get me out of this mess." The Lord says, "Let Me in on this mess." While we are saying, "Deliver me from this situation," the Spirit is praying, "Perfect her in this situation. She needs it for a while longer."

In her multiplied trials, the friend in the Philippines I mentioned earlier has grown to reflect Christ more deeply. She has been stripped of supports in order to find the Rock supporting her in every way. Recently she wrote,

> I see the power of Christ to allow Him to root out all the little fine roots [of things in her life that God doesn't want there]; the big tap root is the "easy" part, the larger feeder roots not so easy, but those fine little hairy ones, left in the ground also produce the same large weed, and MUST go. I spent a long time with Jesus today, more tears, but also felt His power in my life, to purify me within.
>
> These seem to be real purging months for me. A real anointing of sorts felt in teaching, and preparation, and then a real struggle within to BE. A tearful desire to be truly changed, consistent, growing in holiness.

She knows now, beyond a doubt, that her joy, security, *life* is found in *God alone*, and her letters reflect that truth.

Tim and Lynn and my friend Sherry have learned that too. And as I observe their lives, they have helped me to experience a God who never makes mistakes; who is training me for a better life and to be a better me; and who reminds me constantly to keep, above all, my focus on Jesus Christ.

My friends, to you, I am everlastingly *grateful*!

CHAPTER 11

THE REASON FOR IT ALL

◆

*I consider that our present sufferings
are not worth comparing with the glory
that will be revealed in us.*
(ROMANS 8:18)

"Oh, no!" I shrieked as the lights went out in my study, snuffing out the whole chapter I had just finished on the computer. Three hours' worth of work gone in a millisecond! And my back was aching.

Then, believe it or not, I started to grin. Because the subject I'd just been writing about concerned the little things that happen to us when no one else is around to observe. Is there a purpose in those small frustrations? Does the promise of Romans 8:28, "In all things God works for the good of those who love him," include electricity that fails for a moment and eradicates several hours' work? Or is this promise valid only for the big traumas of life?

This question plagued me for years. But in 1985

God showed me a new truth, one that caused me to smile (after a minute) when the electricity failed.

◆ ◆ ◆

Sunday, June 2, 1985, sparkled. After church, we picked up Wendy's hamburgers, and I settled down in my favorite chair to read the Sunday paper. This headline grabbed my attention, causing me to read the following article:

BOY DIES IN ARMS OF MOTHER

Sandra Stahlsmith, four months pregnant with her sixth child, was huddled against the fruit cellar wall, cradling her 6-year-old son Luke in her arms when the tornado struck.

"The wall caved in and it felt like the whole house crashed down on us. I felt my little boy being crushed. He took two breaths and I knew he was dead," Mrs. Stahlsmith said Saturday.

"He died in my arms. It was so tragic. I'll never sleep again," she said, fighting back tears.

Mrs. Stahlsmith was pinned for 30 minutes before neighbors dug her out. She was treated at a nearby hospital for bruises. Her four other children escaped injury.

"His head was resting right on my chin. I could smell his hair. I tried so hard to pick up that wall with my back. I couldn't move a muscle. I thought I was going to die," the 35-year-old woman said.[1]

All week a lump clogged my throat as I thought of that woman, her face buried in her son's hair, knowing the life was gone from his body. And way down deep inside me, I whispered, "Why?"

One month before, I listened as a friend told me of his elderly father's suicide and a terrible accident involving his son-in-law who had fallen sixty feet and landed on his head and face while rock-climbing. The fall resulted in surgeries and impairment for life. And in my heart, I whispered, "Why?"

If you had been standing by Mrs. Stahlsmith or listening to my friend telling of his father and son-in-law, what would you have said? Perhaps, even more importantly, if *your* son died or was impaired permanently, *what would you tell yourself?*

At first, you might be numb, shocked, confused. God might seem silent for some time. But then, the questions would begin to loom large in your distress and grief. "What could possibly be the reason for this terrible tragedy?" you would query. Or, "Is there any reason?"

Then a friend, trying to help, might say, "It's terrible, I know. But remember all things do work together for good for those who love God." You look at her blankly and say nothing. But in your heart, you ask, "How? How can this possibly be good? And for whom?"

I've struggled and ached over the reasons people propose for pain. One heard frequently is, "This is of Satan. God never intended it to happen." An extension might be, "If you had prayed harder, it needn't have happened."

To people who say that I want to yell, "You mean it's *my fault*? You mean Satan has more power than God? You mean Romans 8:28 should read, 'And we know that in all things God works for the good of those who love Him if you've prayed hard enough against the enemy'? But that negates the Word of God. How can you say that?"

Another rationale is, "God didn't cause this. He just permitted it." I try to shake the confusion from my head when I hear that one. I may partially agree with this statement, though I would restate it to say, "God *may not* have caused this." But even if I agree with it as it stands, I'm not sure how much comfort it is or what real bearing it has on a painful situation. If I see my small daughter about to touch a hot stove and I don't prevent her from touching it, am I not responsible for her injury? I didn't *cause it*, but I could have *prevented it*. So how does it help to know God "just permitted it"?

In my opinion, God's sovereignty is at stake here. If certain events or problems come into my life that are not God's plan for me, then those occurrences happen because either God isn't powerful enough to stop them or big enough to know what's going on or caring enough to be interested in the details of my life. But when any of those ideas creep into my thoughts, I go to Psalm 139 and read it again. Look at a few of the verses:

> O Lord, you have examined my heart and know everything about me. . . . You chart the path ahead of me. . . . Every moment, you know where I am. . . . You saw me before I was born and scheduled each day of my life before I began to breathe. Every day was recorded in your Book! How precious it is, Lord, to realize that you are thinking about me constantly! I can't even count how many times a day your thoughts turn towards me. (verses 1,3,16-18; TLB)

You see, GOD "has showered down upon us the richness of his grace—for how well he understands us and knows what is best for us at all times" (Ephesians 1:8, TLB). He is always awake, always watching out for us, always loving us, always doing what is best for us. Of that we can be sure.

In God's sovereignty, He sees the arrow of the enemy hurtling toward me. God could throw up a higher guard to ward it from me. But in His wisdom, He knows that this hard thing is necessary to form patience in my life. So God relaxes His guard and lets the arrow strike me just as He did with Job of old. When pain squeezes the breath of joy from me, when unexplainable trials crowd into my life, I can know for certain that whatever happens to me has God's hand on it.

Now it is true that God never tempts us to do evil. However to equate evil with suffering is to negate the very cross of our Lord. Hebrews 12:1-11 is a graphic description of the endurance of Christ on the cross. That same passage makes application to us and gives us one reason for suffering: "Because the Lord disciplines those he loves, and he punishes everyone he accepts as a son" (verse 6). In Philippians 1:29, Paul said it has been *granted* to us on behalf of Christ to suffer for Him. And yes, it is for our *good*.

I used to tell myself, "I can't know now *how* this is working for good, but in eternity I will find out." That may be true, but must we wait for eternity to know how things work for good? I don't think so anymore.

Another friend responds, "This tragedy is going to bring glory to God as lives are touched and some come to know Christ." This is undoubtedly the case in the final analysis of the major happenings in life, but is this the good talked about in Romans 8:28?

How does that apply to three hours of computer work wiped out by failed electricity, a flat tire on a deserted road, a clothesline collapsing with freshly laundered sheets on it?

Questions. Do I have questions!

In early 1985 God did something He had never done before in my life. In the course of reading through the Bible, He put a "STOP AND GO BACK" sign at the end of Romans 8, which hung there for three months until the truths of that incredible chapter not only moved from my mind to my heart but also began to be absorbed by the fabric of my life. And God began to answer my pleading questions.

The truth of Romans 8 is invalid to an unbeliever. God's promise that everything will work together for good is conditional. The first condition is that this promise is only for "those who love him, who have been called according to his purpose" (verse 28).

I had to stop there. Does this mean the promise is true only for *certain* Christians? Only for those who love God *sufficiently*? To those who are especially called? Is it limiting in its scope even for Christians or is this promise applicable to all Christians?

Have all Christians been called according to His purpose? The fantastic answer is yes! Romans 8:3-4 reads,

> For what the law was powerless to do in that it was weakened by the sinful nature, God did by sending his own Son in the likeness of sinful man to be a sin offering. And so he condemned sin in sinful man in order that the righteous requirements of the law might be fully met in us.

Does that grab you by the shoulders and slam its truth all the way to the bottoms of your feet? My friends, we may not at all times be following His purpose, but every one of us who are Christ-ones have been *called to His purpose*. Every one of us has met His requirements for righteousness, because Christ became the sin offering for us. This truth is meant for each and every believer.

Is the truth invalid if I deliberately disobey? Well, I can thwart God's purpose for my life by disobedience surely. But the moment I confess, I will be thrust right back into the middle of this promise.

What then is the "good" for which all things work together? Can I claim that I'll have a loving husband? Surely that is good. Or children who turn out well? That has got to be good. Or health, a satisfying job, enough money to make me happy? Those things are good, aren't they?

Friend, that sometimes is man's definition of good, but it is never God's.

The ultimate good—the good that shines above everything else God wants us to have—is explained to us by God Himself in the next verse. Why hadn't I seen it? I had known it in my mind years before this, but the truth had not dropped squarely into my life. In Romans 8:29 we read, "For those God foreknew he also predestined to be conformed to the likeness of his Son."

The ultimate good is *not* happiness in this life . . . *not* that souls will rush to know the Savior . . . *not* even that finally Christ will be more glorified (though these things may result). No. *The good* that Romans 8:28 is talking about is that *we be like Jesus*. Fashioned in His image. Conformed to be like Him. To paraphrase it: All things work together for the ultimate good purpose of *making us like Jesus.*

The story is told of an overweight woman who went to a diet center. After weighing her, the director took her to a mirror and on the mirror outlined her figure in the proportions he wanted her to be. Weeks of intense dieting and exercise followed, and weekly (and no doubt weakly!) she would stand in front of that mirror, discouraged because her ample proportions wouldn't fit within the confines of the silhouette. So with renewed determination, she dieted and exercised until one day, standing before that mirror, she was *conformed to its image.*

We will never be conformed to the image of Christ totally until we reach glory. But He is in the business of helping us shape up.

There may be many other reasons for the pain and suffering in our lives, but this is the ultimate one. In some cases, as with the electricity going off in my study, it may be the *only* one. If so, it is enough.

After he lost his dear wife to cancer, Dr. James Means explains in *A Tearful Celebration*:

> Nowhere in the Bible could I find an absolute guarantee of pleasant circumstances. Christians, like others, are subject to sickness, accident, and incalculable loss. If I think God will always keep me comfortable, I am going to feel let down. God will not always do it. Christians are not exempt from trouble.
>
> The true Christian teaching is: "Our present sufferings are not worth comparing with the glory that will be revealed in us" (Romans 8:18). Peter wrote: "Do not be surprised at the painful trial you are suffering, as though something strange were happening to you" (1 Peter 4:12).

I must refuse to be deluded into thinking that
life here and now is a wonderful life. The
wonderful life is the one to come after this one
is over.[2]

Not long ago, a friend said to me, "God isn't
working out His promises in my life."

When I asked her to explain, she said, "God has
promised to give us all good things, hasn't He? Well, I
have been praying for months that He would give me
a nice Christian husband, and He hasn't done it."

I shook my head. "Friend," I responded, "let's
take a look at that verse for what it really says, not
what you are wanting it to say," and we looked at
Romans 8:32 together. "He who did not spare His
own Son, but gave Him up for us all—how will he not
also, along with him, graciously give us all things?"

"See," she interrupted. "God says He will give me
all things, and a Christian husband is the only thing
I'm praying for."

"Let's look at the rest of the chapter," I challenged. "God may define the 'all things' for us."

And He did! The "all things" are defined as three
great truths that should make our hearts shout hallelujah! Because from now through all time and eternity
no one can bring any charge against us (see verse 33).
As awful as we are, as neglectful as we are, as unloving
as we are, *no one* can bring any charge against us because it is God who justifies, and He has justified us!

Second, no one can condemn us! "Christ Jesus,
who died—more than that, who was raised to life—is
at the right hand of God and is also interceding for
us" (verse 34).

Third, nothing and no one can separate us from
God's love in Christ. Neither good things (angels, life,

future) nor bad things (demons, famine, trouble). Nothing in all creation can separate us from the love of God (see verses 35-39). Fantastic!

Of course, many other good things are spelled out for us in Scripture, many of which are right in this chapter. We are delivered from fear (see verse 15); we are heirs of Heaven and have the same inheritance as the Son (see verse 17); we have the Holy Spirit to help us and intercede for us (see verse 26); we are going to have resurrected bodies (see verse 11). Some of these promises are conditional, but a number are unconditional as well. These are the "good things" of time and eternity. When we try to make God's promises fit *our* definition, we are in trouble.

Oh, remember that, dear Christian. The *good things* are: no charge against us, no condemnation for us, no separation from God's love. And *the ultimate good* God is working toward is that we be like Jesus.

What should our response be to this process of being conformed?

First, we must recognize that this painful process is from God and should be something we expect. Life is difficult. To expect a life of ease, comfort, and untarnished happiness is to be unknowledgeable of the purpose of our existence on earth.

Second, we must realize that being conformed is a process, one that cannot be hurried. The story is told of a student who asked the president of his school whether he could take a shorter course than the one prescribed. "Oh, yes," replied the president, "but then it depends on what you want to be. When God wants to make an oak, He takes one hundred years, but when He wants to make a squash, He takes six months."

Third, we must realize that our wills are involved.

A friend of mine made this pithy observation: "The Holy Spirit does not come into our lives to do His deepest work in our shallowest part—our feelings. But He comes into our lives to do His deepest work in our deepest part—our wills."

She added, "Many mornings we may not *feel* like getting up to spend time with the Lord. But it is our choice—our will—to get up."

Fourth, we must keep looking up and ahead to the future. We must ask God to help us keep eternity in mind and heart, to put a glad hand around our emotions so that we will realize with joy and delight that the creation itself will clap its hands when the sons of God are revealed (see Romans 8:19-22). We must not forget that soon we will experience the redemption of our bodies (see verses 23-25), and that not only in the future but right this minute, God is for us! He loves us! Nothing on earth or above the earth or below the earth can pry us loose from His love.

A gold refiner remarked to a group of women who had just completed their tour through the refinery, "The refiner can tell when the refining process is complete when he can see his reflection in the finished product." When we hang on to that we will let go of our whys.

I loved the following thoughts that Ruth Graham expressed in *It's My Turn*:

I lay my "why's"
before Your Cross
in worship kneeling,
my mind too numb
for thought,
my heart beyond
all feeling:

And worshipping,
realize that I
in knowing You
don't need a "why."[3]

Our granddaughter Sunny said it well: "My life hurts more than my leg." When God strips us, our whole life, not just an injured and hurting extremity, throbs with pain.

Many missing pieces in the puzzle of life remain firmly clasped in the Father's hand. Yet there is *one* reason for all the events that happen to us, for the stripping processes that shape our lives. We can grip this truth with determination and faith: Everything that comes into our lives is for the ultimate good of making us like Jesus. Everything.

Believe it.

Because . . . it's true!

NOTES:
1. *Gazette Telegraph*, Colorado Springs, Colo., June 2, 1985.
2. James Means, *A Tearful Celebration* (Portland: Multnomah, 1985), page 18.
3. Ruth Graham Bell, *It's My Turn* (Old Tappan, N.J.: Revell, 1982), page 169.

PERSONAL APPLICATION
AND REFLECTION

CHAPTER 1
Abject Failure: Losing Success

1. Have you ever felt like a failure? Do you think God allowed you to fail? What did you learn or what are you learning through this experience?
2. Write out 2 Timothy 2:11-13 in your own words.
   a. What do these verses say to you?
   b. How have you experienced the faithfulness of God?
   c. How have you experienced the faithfulness of God when you have been unfaithful to Him?
3. a. What brings you delight?
   b. Look up the following verses and summarize from each that in which we should delight: Nehemiah 1:11; Psalm 35:9, 43:4, 111:2, 112:1; Proverbs 8:30; 2 Corinthians 12:9-10.

4. a. List three of your strengths and three of your weaknesses.
   b. What have you learned about God through your strengths? Through your weaknesses?
5. Write a brief letter to the Lord based on the above study.

CHAPTER 2
Waiting in the Fog: Losing Sight

1. a. In one paragraph summarize Philippians 4:4-7.
   b. Write out Philippians 4:6 in your own words. Don't condense it but amplify its meaning, including your own interpretation.
2. Using a concordance, find two verses that shed light on the word *anxious* and two verses about *thanksgiving.*
3. a. List concerns you have right now, putting the greatest concern first.
   b. Place a check next to those concerns in which you can take action.
   c. Read Matthew 11:28-30 and take a few minutes to pray, offering your list of concerns to the Father. Now ask Him for the strength to do what you can do with the ones you have checked for action and for the grace to *leave* the others in His hand.
4. a. Read Psalm 11 out loud, emphasizing the verbs (including the verb *is*). Then fill in the following outline:
      I. Where the Lord is.
      II. Characteristics of the Lord (or *who* the Lord is).
      III. What the Lord is doing.
      IV. My response to the Lord.
   b. Are the facts about God stated above less true when we are in a fog of waiting? What steps can I take to remain steadfast even in the fog?

CHAPTER 3
When All Props Go: Losing Support Systems

1. Read Psalm 66 in two or three versions of the Bible. If you have only one version, read it three times. List the ways the psalmist praises God in this psalm. (One example: "Shout with joy" [verse 1].)

2. Psalm 66 was written *after* God had delivered David, but let's take a look at David's response *during* a time when men were conspiring against him.

   a. Read Psalm 55 and list the negative emotions expressed there.

   b. List the positive steps the psalmist took in the midst of his trouble. (One example: He prayed [verses 16-17].)

3. Read Psalm 62.

   a. List the "alones" or "onlys" in this psalm.

   b. Complete this statement honestly: My soul finds rest in God and _____ .

4. a. Using a concordance, look up two verses on God's *strength* and two verses on His *love*.

   b. How should His strength and love affect us in our everyday lives?

   c. What steps can you take this week to let the truth of His strength and love become more real in your life?

CHAPTER 4

Inexplicable Incapacitation: Losing Strength

1. Read Psalm 73.
    a. In two or three paragraphs and in first person, paraphrase how the psalmist felt as revealed in verses 1-22. (One example: "Help! I'm slipping, Lord!")
    b. Read verses 23-28 and write one paragraph in first person telling what the psalmist determined. (One example: "Lord, I know You're holding me tight!")
2. As you read Psalm 51:10-12, stop after these four words and think about them: *create, renew, restore, grant*. List what you need from God in relation to each of these verbs and pray about each need.

CHAPTER 5

Character Assassination: Losing Self

Do you know how to do a character study? They can be both fun and meaningful. I suggest you do one this week on Joseph. Here's how:

1. Read the portion of Scripture that tells of Joseph's life, Genesis 37-50. (I know that is thirteen chapters, but it won't take long, honest!) As you read, take notes concerning the character traits of Joseph (jot chapter and verse alongside each note) and your interpretation of the events as well as factual information about Joseph's life. (Examples of factual information: Joseph was the son of _____; when he was seventeen he _____. Example of interpretive information: At first, Joseph revealed some pride.)

2. Write a one-page summary of Joseph's life (not more than three hundred words), using both factual information and your interpretations.

3. Write one paragraph on what you consider the most outstanding characteristic of Joseph's life.

4. a. What was Joseph's response to his difficulties?
   b. Why do you think this is true?

5. Pray about what you studied. How do you think God wants you to apply what you have learned?

◆ ◆ ◆

To do other character studies, use the above outline (except for question four). You can study any character in the Bible this way, except perhaps the major ones such as David or Paul. Studying biblical characters is a wonderful way to learn doctrines such as prayer (Hannah), being versus doing (Mary and Martha), and others.

CHAPTER 6
Aloneness: Losing Intimacy

A topical Bible study is another type that can be meaningful. If you have never done one, you have a new treat in store for you. A topical study can be as short or as extensive as you want to make it. Let me give you seven steps that can be used for any topical study, either a word study or a subject study, as the basis of a sermon or talk or for personal Bible study. The first letter of each step spells TOPICAL:

T — Title
O — Outline
P — Problems
I — Illustrations
C — Commentaries
A — Application
L — List of verses for future memorization

Now let's do a short topical study of Scripture. This time I will give you the verses to look up, but in the future, you can take any word or phrase, look it up in a concordance, select twenty to twenty-five verses and go from there. This time we will do only the title, outline, and application steps. You can follow all seven steps in future topical studies.
1. Title: Fear
2. Outline: Look up the following verses, write them out, and then outline them: Psalm 27:1-3, 46:1-2, 112:7-8; Isaiah 41:10, 43:1-3; 1 John 4:18. Here are two sample outlines:

    I. God's Part
    A. His characteristics

   B. His ministry
 II. My Part
   A. My responsibility
   B. Specific actions to take

   I. Who God Is
  II. What God Does
 III. Situations Not to Fear
 IV. Reasons Not to Fear

3. Application: What fears am I facing? What action should I take in the light of one or more of these verses?

If you want to study further, do a brief topical study on the word *afraid* using 2 Chronicles 20:17; Psalm 56:3-4,11; John 14:27; Hebrews 13:5-6.

CHAPTER 7
In the Valley of the Shadow: Losing Loved Ones

1. Write out a dictionary definition of *death*.
2. How do you imagine God might define *death* for a Christian?
3. Read slowly 1 Corinthians 15:35-58.
   a. Paraphrase verses 42-43, noting the contrasts.
   b. Have you ever heard the phrase "O death, where is your sting?" used to comfort someone who has lost a loved one? Carefully read verses 51-56 again. When will death lose its sting? (See verse 54. Note: Christians are sometimes made to feel guilty when they grieve over the death of a loved one. Often verse 55 is taken out of context. The passage is saying there is a sting in death *now*, but in the future, death will lose its sting.)
   c. Write in your own words Paul's concluding statement in verse 58. What is to be our mission? For how long?
4. Optional study: Look up the words *death* and *grave* in a concordance. Select three or four verses for each word, and do a brief topical study using them (see format from topical study, chapter 6).

CHAPTER 8
The Coming of Winter: Losing Youth

1. Paraphrase Psalm 71:9.
2. What do you think some of the ministries of older people are in light of these verses: Psalm 71:18, 101:2; 1 Corinthians 15:58; Philippians 1:20-21; Titus 2:4-5.
3. What should be our attitude toward death in light of these verses: Psalm 116:15, Romans 8:18-25, 1 Corinthians 15:42-44.
4. Read slowly Colossians 1:9-12.
   a. Write out the verbs of actions Paul used when praying for the Colossians. (One example: "to fill" [verse 9].)
   b. Summarize in one paragraph the quality of life Paul and others prayed for these people to have.
   c. List the *key ingredients* inherent to this kind of life. How are those qualities obtained according to this and related passages? (Note: one quality is the knowledge of God's will [see verse 9]. How do we get that knowledge? This verse tells us we get it "through all spiritual wisdom." How do we get spiritual wisdom and understanding? To answer this, you will have to use other Scriptures such as Proverbs 2:1-6 and Ephesians 3:14-19.)
5. Based on the passage in Colossians 1, what one thing would God have you do to prepare for the rest of your life?

CHAPTER 9
Desolation: Losing the Sense of God's Presence

1. Read Psalm 16:5.
   a. List some of the ingredients making up your "portion." Have you resented any part of that portion? Why?
   b. What factors are included in your "cup"? (List some of your sorrows, joys, and routines of daily life.) Which of these have you drunk of fully? Which have been hard for you to partake of fully? Why? What could you do to experience your life's cup more fully?
2. Read Lamentations 3.
   a. List three or four factors from verses 1-18 with which you especially identify. Have those experiences in your life caused resentment or growth for you?
   b. Take a moment right now to remember what God has done for you in the last ten years.
3. a. List two of your strengths and two of your weaknesses.
   b. What have you learned about God through your strengths? Through your weaknesses?
4. In a practical way, how is God your *portion*? (See Psalm 142:5.) What does this mean to you?

CHAPTER 10
Trials upon Trials: Losing Understanding

1. Read Hebrews 12:1-12.
   a. List what the passage says about training (some translations use the word *discipline*), both human training and God's training.
   b. What hinders God's training process in our lives? What ways can we block God's training? Which ways have *you* used to block His training?
2. In the *New International Version*, verse 5 reads: "And you have forgotten that *word of encouragement* that addresses you as sons: 'My son, do not make light of the Lord's discipline'" (italics mine).
   a. How is discipline an *encouragement*?
   b. Is it hard for you to think of discipline as God's encouragement? Why?
   c. What could you do to begin to think of God's discipline in a more positive light? (For instance, you might do a topical study on the reasons Christians suffer.)
3. In Hebrews 12:16 *The Living Bible* uses the phrase "careless about God" (NIV: "godless").
   a. What are some ways Christians are "careless about God"?
   b. List two ways you sometimes are careless about Him?
   c. What can you do to become more *careful*, instead of careless, in certain areas of your life?

CHAPTER 11
The Reason for It All

Let's learn to do a chapter study—in this case a portion of a chapter. This is the "meat and potatoes" of Bible study. A simple format consists of four questions.

What does the chapter say?
What does it say that I don't understand?
What do related passages say about the chapter?
What does the chapter say to me?

Read carefully and prayerfully Romans 8:28-39 at least three times.

1. What do these verses say? Either outline or paraphrase the passage.

2. What does the passage say that I don't understand? Write out any questions you have about words or thoughts. (For those who have done this kind of study before, go a step further and find the *answers* to your questions. Some may be answered by other Scriptures, so you may want to wait until the next step. But come back and answer your questions as fully as possible. Use a good commentary only as a last resort. Don't become dependent on someone else's thoughts before you really pray and work to find your own solutions.)

3. What do related Scriptures say about the passage? You need a good concordance for this to look up key words and phrases. Or find Scriptures that *illustrate* by example the truth expressed by a verse in the passage. Or *contrast* a thought from the passage with other Scriptures.

4. What does the passage say to me? Write out your own personal application using the following guidelines:
   a. Write out one verse God is especially speaking to you about.
   b. Write how you are failing to obey this verse.
   c. Give a specific example of failure to obey.
   d. After praying, list what God wants you to do to correct your failure *this week*. Be specific about this. (Examples: Put it at the top of your prayer list and memorize the verse God is speaking to your heart about. If at all possible, ask someone to hold you accountable at the end of the week.)